T0311392

Friendship and
Social Media

Friendship is regarded as crucial to living a good life. But how does friendship make our lives better? Do all friendships make our lives better? What sorts of interactions are necessary for maintaining valuable friendships?

This book answers these questions via a philosophical exploration of friendship and the ways that it contributes value to our lives. Diane Jeske uses this philosophical analysis to assess the impact of our ever-growing use of social media: Do interactions via social media interfere with our ability to maintain genuine friendships? Do such interactions undermine the contribution of friendship to the value of our lives?

In addressing these topics, Jeske examines the contemporary notion of a 'frenemy,' the ways in which we deliberately craft our social media personas, the role of the physical body in friendship, and the ways in which social media's exacerbation of our fear of being left out and of comparison-based envy can impact our relationships.

Written in a clear and engaging style, Friendship and Social Media brings philosophical rigor and clarity to the task of determining how we can responsibly use social media in our own lives. It is essential reading for anyone interested in the ethics of interpersonal relationships and the social impact of technology.

Diane Jeske is Professor of Philosophy at the University of Iowa, USA. She is the author of *Rationality and Moral Theory: How Intimacy Generates Reasons* (Routledge, 2008) and *The Evil Within: Why We Need Moral Philosophy* (2018). With Richard Fumerton she is editor of *Introducing Philosophy Through Film* (2010) and *Readings in Political Philosophy: Theory and Applications* (2012).

DIANE JESKE

Friendship and
Social Media

A Philosophical Exploration

Routledge
Taylor & Francis Group

LONDON AND NEW YORK

First published 2019
by Routledge
2 Park Square, Milton Park, Abingdon, Oxon OX14 4RN

and by Routledge
52 Vanderbilt Avenue, New York, NY 10017

Routledge is an imprint of the Taylor & Francis Group, an informa business

British Library Cataloguing-in-Publication Data
A catalogue record for this book is available from the British Library

Library of Congress Cataloging-in-Publication Data
Names: Jeske, Diane, 1967– author.
Title: Friendship and social media: a philosophical exploration / Diane Jeske.
Description: Abingdon, Oxon; New York, NY: Routledge is an imprint of the
Taylor & Francis Group, an Informa Business, 2019. | Includes bibliographical
references and index.
Identifiers: LCCN 2018039705| ISBN 9781138629448 (hbk: alk. paper) | ISBN
9781138387409 (pbk: alk. paper) | ISBN 9781315210452 (ebk)
Subjects: LCSH: Friendship. | Social media.
Classification: LCC BF575.F66 .J47 2019 | DDC 177/.62—dc23
LC record available at https://lccn.loc.gov/2018039705

ISBN: 978-1-138-62944-8 (hbk)
ISBN: 978-1-138-38740-9 (pbk)
ISBN: 978-1-315-21045-2 (ebk)

Typeset in Joanna
by codeMantra

For Richard: Colleague, Mentor, Friend

Contents

Preface: friendship, philosophy, and Facebook   ix

Friendship and the good life   One   1

Connecting friendship and the good life   4
The value of friendship   10
Friendship and morality   13
Value, happiness, and welfare   19

The nature of friendship   Two   25

Caring for another for her own sake   28
Self-revelation and friendship   35
Spending time with our friends   40
Love and affection   48
Friendship as intimacy   50
The reasons of friendship   57
Friends, lovers, and other relations   60

Friendship online   Three   65

Making and keeping friends on social media   65
Reading our friends   70
Responding and caring   75
Love and affection in digital space   81
Maintaining a unique bond   85

What good are friends? **Four** **89**

Value and its incarnations 91

The consequences of friendship 97

Desire-Satisfaction and friends 110

Friendship as objectively intrinsically valuable 117

Friendship, virtue, and the good life 125

Friendship and rationality 128

Social media and the value of friendship **Five** **133**

Getting good results on Facebook 135

The subjective and objective intrinsic value
of friendship 148

Being cautious 154

Index **157**

Preface
Friendship, philosophy, and Facebook

Every year we are living more and more of our life online: we shop on the internet, we stream movies, videos, and games, we read and create blogs, we communicate with each other via Skype and e-mail, we teach and take courses online, we search for information using Google and Bing, and we update our own and visit other people's Facebook pages. There are, of course, positive aspects of these changes: we can keep in closer and more regular touch with friends who live far away, we have access to many resources that were previously unavailable, such as products and information, and we have new avenues for entertainment and education.

But as technology sweeps us along in its fast-paced, ever-expanding dominance over our lives, we need to find opportunities to pause and to reflect on the ways in which that technology is altering how we spend our time and how we interact with each other, so that we can resist negative changes and put forth effort to preserve valuable aspects of our lives and relationships that are being threatened.

Most people would agree that our friendships are among the most important parts of our lives, and also that technology is having a serious impact not only on how we conduct these relationships but also on how we conceptualize the very nature of friendship. Facebook has famously, or, perhaps more accurately, infamously, co-opted the term 'friend' in such a way that people now brag about the number of such friends that they have (usually somewhere over 100) and have the power to instantaneously 'friend' or 'defriend' someone. People are not only initiating relationships online but are sometimes using social media and the like as the primary mode of interacting with those with whom they have formed (or reignited) relationships.

In a recent book on friendship, Alexander Nehamas distinguishes between "close friendship" and "the indiscriminate kind that is so easily forged through Facebook."[1] Nehamas's remark leaves it unclear whether he thinks there is some new kind of friendship available to Facebook users, that what is happening on Facebook is a debased form of the familiar type of friendship, or that what is transpiring on Facebook is something altogether of a different kind from traditional friendship. In order to categorize what is happening on Facebook, we need to examine our traditional concept of friendship and the possibilities for its enactment via social media. It is imperative that we reflect on and clarify what it means for two people to be friends so that we can resist conflation of genuine friendship with new-fangled knock-offs, and also to ensure that we do not lose what matters about the former.

I hope that this book serves as just such an opportunity to reflect on the nature of friendship and the ways in which our friendships are being altered, for better or for worse, by online activities, in particular by social media such as Facebook. For most of us, friendships play a central role in our life plans, so we need to reflect on the ways in which we conduct those relationships. Further, we have to reflect on the new ways that we form and maintain relationships, to ask whether relationships formed in these ways are genuine friendships, and – whether they are or not – to consider if such relationships are doing us harm, perhaps by usurping the role of more traditional relationships in our lives.

But of course these reflections on friendship need to occur in the broader context of reflecting on what is good for us and how friendship promotes that good. Too often in philosophical discussions of friendship, it is simply taken for granted that friendship is an essential part of a good life without any claims about how we are to understand the nature of the good life or the role that friendship plays in it. So this book puts friendship into the context of a valuable life as a whole in order to see how adding social media into the mix might alter the overall picture. Although my focus is on only one type of interpersonal relationship, namely friendship, I think that what I say has implications for our use of online technologies in other sorts of relationships, too, such as that between teacher and student or between doctor and patient.

The book is structured as follows: In Chapter One, various important distinctions are made that are crucial to understanding the nature of the project. We need to determine what questions we are asking about friendship and the good life, and to clarify some of the concepts involved in those questions and their answers.

Chapter Two offers an exploration of some features of interpersonal relationships that have been taken as part of the friendship relationship and a defense of my own view of friendship, which understands that relationship in very expansive terms. I will use the contemporary notion of a 'frenemy' to illustrate these features of friendship and also to show how capacious our concept of friendship really is.

In Chapter Three I consider how these features of friendships might be affected by the usage of social media to maintain the friendship. While how friendship is affected by social media will differ from one relationship to another, I think that we can locate some worries and challenges that Facebook and Twitter pose to the maintenance of intimate, caring relationships.

Chapters Four and Five then turn to the issue of how friendship and social media fit into the good life for a human person. In Chapter Four I explore the ways in which friendship contributes value to our lives. Chapter Five then suggests some ways in which social media usage or, at least, overuse of social media might interfere with the production of such value, either by blocking or diminishing some of the standard good consequences of friendship or by altering or weakening some of the components of friendship itself.

My overall conclusion with respect to using social media to maintain friendships is that we need to be cautious and wary about how we go about it. Social media, like much modern technology, is not particularly conducive to honest, heartfelt reflection and self-examination. My hope, then, is that the discussions in the following chapters provide a space for you to sit back and reflect on your own relationships and how social media is impacting them, and thus impacting the quality of your own life and the quality of the lives of the people you love.

Philosophical investigation involves the examination of our concepts and the connections between those concepts. It provides us a framework for approaching more empirical investigations about the impact of social media on our lives and relationships. Philosophy also requires and calls forth the kind of honest self-examination that we need if we are to approach social media employment in friendships in a meaningful and productive way. It is imperative that we do this so that we do not wake up one day and realize that we have lost the best parts of our lives through careless use of whatever the latest technologies happened to be.

I would like to thank my editor at Routledge, Tony Bruce, for suggesting the idea for this book and for supporting it through the process to publication. I received three anonymous reports on the proposal for the book and three anonymous reports on the first draft of the manuscript, and I would like to thank the authors of those reports for the helpful comments and critique that certainly improved the final product. Finally, I would like to thank Richard Fumerton, to whom I dedicate this book, for his constant support and friendship over the course of my career.

NOTE

1 Alexander Nehamas, *On Friendship* (New York, NY: Basic Books, 2016): 4.

Friendship and the good life
One

Imagine that you are an expert in the newly emerged field of 'non-Earth living' and have been hired to spend two years on another planet, preparing it for future colonization. Those in charge of the mission give you some options. First, they ask whether you would like to spend the two years on this planet by yourself or whether you would like to have a companion go with you. I am confident that virtually anyone would choose to have some company rather than to spend two years alone. Then the mission organizers say that you can choose between two companions: both are trained in 'non-Earth living,' but one is a close friend and the other is someone you have never met. Again, the choice seems obvious: the company of a friend, particularly a close friend, is surely preferable to that of a stranger.

Our responses to this thought experiment provide support for two distinct claims. First, most of us regard being alone for significant portions of our lives as somehow bad, something to be avoided. Second, we think that such solitude is best addressed by the company of friends as opposed to the company of strangers; in fact, it may be that the pains of such solitude can only be alleviated by being in the company of friends. Aristotle famously claimed that "no one would choose to live without friends even if he had all the other goods."[1]

Most people, I think, would agree with Aristotle: no matter how much money, how much power, how much fame, how much success we might have, it would not compensate us for a lack of friends in our lives. Friendship, then, seems to play, at least for most of us, an important role in our conception of what it is to live a good or worthwhile life.

But what is it to be 'in the company of' our friends? What exactly counts as 'living without friends'? For previous generations, non-face-to-face contact with friends could take place only via written letters or the telephone, with the latter often being a costly and thus rationed mode of communication with distant friends. In any case, if our friends were not physically proximate to us, contact was only intermittent. But this has changed entirely. We carry our phones with us, and we can use those phones not only to talk with friends but to e-mail them, to send instant text messages to them, and to post thoughts and pictures to Twitter, Instagram, and Facebook. We can Skype with our friends, thereby having online conversations where we can see our friends in real-time. Thus, even if one were to take up one's post on a distant planet while one's friend remained on Earth, one could be in almost constant contact with that friend (as long as the technology was enabled).

Nonetheless, I know that I would greatly prefer that my good friend be able to physically accompany me on my interplanetary mission, and I expect that most of my readers will share such a preference.[2] When communicating with friends via social media, e-mail, or even Skype, we often stress to those we have not seen in a while that we miss them and really wish that we could get together, that we could *be* together. Why is this? What, if anything, is missing from interactions that are not face-to-face?

Facebook has found itself at the heart of much of the current debate about the role of technology in conducting interpersonal relationships including, most prominently, friendship. Facebook itself has co-opted the term 'friend': one can 'friend' (or, of course, 'defriend') people, thereby granting (or denying) them the ability to view one's posts and to respond to those posts in various ways. According to one 2012 source, the average Facebook user has 245 'friends.'[3] Of course, this is a number of people such that one could never get together with all of them on anything like a regular basis, and most people recognize that the Facebook notion of a 'friend' is not our ordinary notion of a friend: not all Facebook 'friends,' in other words, are 'really' our friends (and, of course, not all of our 'real' friends are Facebook 'friends'). Nonetheless, Facebook is playing a significant role in many relationships, and scholars in various disciplines have begun to wonder whether this is a fact to be celebrated or lamented (or, perhaps, both).

The philosopher has not only an important but a fundamental role in any attempt to address these issues. After all, if we are to understand the results of any empirical studies, we need to understand what makes a relationship a genuine friendship, what sorts of things make our lives go well, and whether and under what conditions friendship can contribute such goods to our lives. The job of the philosopher is to analyze what we mean when we talk about friendship, what we mean when we talk about living well, and then to explain the nature of the actual and potential connections between friendship and the goods of human life.

But, of course, we do not want to assume from the outset that friendship only contributes good things to our lives. The title of Carole King's famous song, "You've Got a Friend," is intended to be a statement of consolation, comfort, and support. But, in some circumstances, it can be a statement encapsulating moral conflict, self-sacrifice, grief, and betrayal. Friendships are complex relationships that are embedded in particular lives in myriad ways, and the contributions that they make to those lives are as various as the people who stand in those relationships and the circumstances in which those people find themselves. Importantly, Facebook and other digital technologies are altering the ways in which friendships are embedded in many lives, and so we need to examine these changes in light of our philosophical understandings of friendship and the good life in order to get a handle on whether we ought to bemoan or to applaud our new ways of interacting.

We can begin by examining the type of connection that it is plausible to suppose exists between friendship and the good life.

1.1 CONNECTING FRIENDSHIP AND THE GOOD LIFE

1.1.1 The concept of necessity

In a recent article on friendship, the authors said "obviously friendship is an important human good."[4] Most of us, I am sure, regard this claim as obviously true. But what do we mean when we attribute such a status to friendship? Do we mean that *any* friend, no matter her character, makes our lives go better? Does a friend make our lives go better no matter what else is true of our lives, i.e. no matter what circumstances we find ourselves in: for example, does it matter whether we already have several or many friends? If friendship makes a contribution to the quality of our lives, what is the nature of that contribution? Does it always make such a contribution? Does it *necessarily* make such a contribution?

Philosophers are often engaged in the study of necessary connections, and so it is natural in a philosophical enquiry of this sort to ask whether such a connection exists between friendship and the good life. But before we can consider this question, we need to understand the concept of necessity.

Suppose that Joe has been studying physics and in reporting what he has learned he says that metal expands when it is heated. Jane asks Joe, "Is it necessary that metal expands when heated?" Joe might then respond, "Yes, it is necessary, because the laws of nature require it." What Joe is pointing out is that our world is governed by certain physical laws, i.e. in our world, certain types of events always cause certain other types of events: for example, the heating of metal always causes that metal to expand. But Jane might push Joe, asking him whether it is necessary that the world be governed by the physical laws by which it is actually governed. In order to prompt Joe to think about this question, she might ask, "Can you coherently imagine that we lived in a world in which metal did not expand when heated?"

Now, of course, if Joe has any imagination at all, he will respond that of course he can imagine such a world. After all, science fiction and fantasy are genres that depend upon the reader being able to conceive of worlds in which the physical laws are quite different than they are in the actual world. Also, if it was necessary that metal expands when heated in the way that it is necessary that $2 + 2 = 4$, then we would never have had to engage in experiments to establish the former any more than we had to engage in experiments to establish the latter. So it is necessary that metal expands when heated only if we assume that the world is governed by the physical laws that hold in the actual world. But it is not necessary, in the sense that we can imagine other possible worlds in which the physical laws are different and so metal does not expand when heated.[5] On the other hand, we cannot conceive of a possible world in which $2 + 2$ does not equal 4: we do not have to hold anything else constant about the world in order for it to be the case that $2 + 2 = 4$.

When philosophers ask whether, for example, it is necessary that a person have only one body throughout her existence, they are asking whether it is the case that *in all possible worlds* a person has only one body throughout her existence. Some philosophers take the talk of possible worlds literally, while others view it merely as a metaphor for understanding how things might be but are not actually. If we want to know whether some state of affairs, though not actual, is possible – "Can I get a new body?" – we sometimes ask ourselves whether that state of affairs is *conceivable* – "Can I coherently imagine myself in a new body?" I can certainly coherently imagine that I have differently colored hair or that I have five children (I actually do not), and I certainly cannot coherently imagine a round square or $2 + 2$ equaling 5. Much philosophical work involves disputes about whether some claim, such as 'a person has only one body throughout her existence,' is a necessary truth. Some of the more controversial cases can only be decided after considerable effort has been expended to understand and clarify the concepts involved.

So necessary truths, as I am understanding the notion of necessity, are truths which hold in all possible worlds, while contingent truths are those that hold only in some possible worlds. Or we can say that necessary truths are ones that we cannot conceive of as false, while contingent truths are such that we can coherently conceive of them as false.[6] Joe's claim that metal expands when heated is a contingent truth, the claim that $2 + 2 = 4$ is a necessary truth, and the claim that a person cannot switch bodies is a claim that some philosophers regard as a necessary truth while others view it as a contingent truth. The dispute about the latter claim arises from philosophical dispute about the concept of a person, i.e. about what it is to be a person and for a person to persist through time. In Chapter Two we will see that Aristotle, for example, claimed that it is impossible for two morally bad people to be friends, while many contemporary philosophers of friendship insist that it is possible for two wicked people to be friends: this is a dispute about what it is for two people to be friends, i.e. about the concept of friendship.

Is it at all plausible to suppose that there is a necessary connection between friendship and the good life?

1.1.2 Friendship, the good life, and necessity

Charlie has no friends. He interacts with people only in so far as is necessary to survive in the modern world. So, for example, he interacts with the cashier at the supermarket, his colleagues at work, the manager of his apartment building, the cable installer, etc. However, all of these interactions are purely utilitarian in nature: he talks to his colleagues only about their joint work projects, to the cashier only about whether he wants paper or plastic, etc. He does not socialize, but, rather, spends all of the time when he is not working or doing things like shopping for groceries in solitary pursuits.

Most people will probably react to Charlie's story in the same way: they will pity him, wonder how his sad existence came to be, and will be glad not to have a life such as Charlie's. Such reactions certainly suggest that we do not regard Charlie as living a good life, and these reactions are the result of the fact that Charlie has no friends. Such reactions, then, also suggest that there is some plausibility to the following claim:

> **Necessity of friends:** Necessarily, if a person lacks friends, then that person is not leading a good life.

But is *Necessity of friends* really plausible? I gave a very sketchy description of Charlie's life. Let's now add some details. Charlie is a team leader at the Center for Disease Control (CDC) and has done critical, life-saving work in stemming and preventing epidemics. He is greatly admired by everyone who works in his field. When he has any free time, he reads extensively in history, fiction, and (of course) philosophy, and goes to museums and to the theater. All of these activities rejuvenate him to return to the CDC and save lives. He has purposely curtailed socializing so that he can focus on his work because he is passionately committed to helping better the condition of other human beings.

Once I have filled out Charlie's story, I think that reactions of pity toward what we previously viewed as a sad existence dissipate. Charlie is engaged in fulfilling, valuable activities that fully engage his considerable leadership and intellectual talents. He is never bored or lonely because he has a sense of purpose and has structured his life so as best to fulfill that genuinely significant purpose. Our change in reaction to the filled-out version of Charlie's story suggests that our inclinations to accept *Necessity of friends* might actually have been the result of supposing that Charlie was lonely and unfulfilled rather than the result of just supposing that Charlie has no friends.

It is certainly the case that most of us would not be happy if we were living a life such as Charlie's, but that seems to be a matter of our psychological make-up, and psychological make-up varies between people. For example, I know that I need the emotional support of friends in order to deal with the stresses of work. However, I have imagined Charlie as being someone who deals with that stress in a solitary but nonetheless successful way. People like Charlie might be rare but it is surely the case that we can conceive of such people, so it does not seem to be a necessary truth that one cannot lead a good life if one has no friends.

However, we might still have the sense that, even if Charlie is living a good life, something important is missing from it, something that would enhance various aspects of it in quite significant ways. Surely, we think, Charlie would be leading an even better life if, say, he were to develop a friendship with one of the members of his CDC team, a friendship that did not detract from his commitment to his work but actually complemented that commitment. This suggests:

> **Better with friends:** Necessarily, if a person has at least one friend, then that person has a better life than she would if she lacked friends (holding everything else about her life constant).

Better with friends is compatible with the denial of Necessity of friends: Better with friends, unlike Necessity of friends, allows that one could lead a good life even if one had no friends, but insists that one would be even better off if one added at least one friend into the mix.

It certainly seems that friendship adds value to a life, but the addition of value is not sufficient for making one's life *overall* better. After all, while friendship often provides us with laughter, support, companionship, and love, there is no doubt that it can also increase our suffering: friends get sick and die, they get depressed, they ask us to help them to move or to drive them to the airport, they engage in actions that we find morally questionable and make us feel tainted by association, or they reveal confidences and betray us for their own advancement. Where the balance lies between the joys of affection and support on the one hand and the suffering induced by loss and betrayal on the other seems to depend upon the nature of a particular friendship and of its circumstances. Charlie might find that befriending his colleague Lucy makes his work more enjoyable and rewarding, but it might also be the case that Lucy ends up dying of one of the epidemics that Charlie struggled to stem, thereby causing him grief that impedes his sense of purpose. So we cannot simply add a friend to a person's life and hold everything else constant: friendships have consequences, both good and bad.

So neither *Necessity of friends* nor *Better with friends* seems plausible in the end. But the rejection of these necessity claims is compatible with the claims that friendship is valuable and that it can contribute value to our lives. However, we need to be careful about how we understand this notion of value.

1.2 THE VALUE OF FRIENDSHIP

Virtually everyone would claim to value their friends and to value their friendships. They would also probably agree to the claim that their friends and their friendships are valuable. These two claims need to be distinguished from one another, and we also need to disambiguate the claim that friendship is valuable.

When I say that I value my friend Isabel and my friendship with her, I am making a psychological claim about my attitudes to Isabel and my relationship with her. I am saying that

I care about Isabel and about our relationship and that it is of importance to me. When I value something, I want to protect and preserve it. When I value someone, I want to nurture and take care of her.

Does the claim that I value my friendship with Isabel imply that my friendship with Isabel is valuable? The answer to this claim depends on what we think it means to say that my friendship is valuable. Some philosophers will answer 'yes' to the question because they believe that when I say that my friendship with Isabel is valuable, I am just saying that I value my friendship with Isabel. For such philosophers, something's being valuable is always a matter of its being valuable for *someone*, i.e. for it to be valued by someone. Other philosophers will answer 'no' to the question because they believe that there is some fact of the matter about something's being valuable that is independent of whether anyone values it. These philosophers will insist that the mere fact that, for example, Isaac values his collection of gum wrappers is not sufficient to render that collection worth valuing: they deny that a collection of gum wrappers is objectively valuable regardless of Isaac's (or anyone else's) attitudes toward that collection. (We will discuss this distinction between objective and subjective value further in Chapter Four.)

But whatever account of the nature of value that we adopt, we need to make the distinction between intrinsic and instrumental value. The notion of instrumental value is parasitic upon that of intrinsic value:

> **Intrinsic value and instrumental value:** To say that X has intrinsic value is to say that X is valuable for its own sake, or as an end. To say that X has instrumental value is to say that X is a means to the production of something that has intrinsic value.

Consider an example: we all want money – the more of it the better, we usually think. But we do not regard money as being good for its own sake: we think that money is good because we can use it to get other things, i.e. it is instrumentally good. If I just had piles of money but no one would let me buy anything, I would not regard my piles of money as good at all (unless I can find some other use for my money, such as using it as a mattress stuffing).

On the other hand, some philosophers such as Plato regard, for example, pleasure as intrinsically good.[7] Pleasure, like money, is one of those things that we all want, the more the better it seems. But pleasure is such that we do still want it, even if we get nothing else as a result. In fact, money often seems good to us because we can use it to buy things that will give us pleasure, things such as chocolate, massages, trips to Las Vegas, etc. And pleasure, unlike money, seems good no matter what else is the case.[8]

An important question about friendship, then, is whether it is intrinsically valuable or merely instrumentally valuable. Often, when we praise friendship, we praise it in terms of the good consequences to which it often leads: we get pleasure from spending time with our friends, our friends give us comfort and support in difficult situations, friends help us move and give us rides to the airport, etc. But of course sometimes friendship seems to have bad consequences: we grieve when our friends die, we have to help them to move and drive them to the airport, friends sometimes reveal confidences or in other ways fail to live up to our expectations of them. Friends are able to hurt our feelings much more deeply than are others because they know us well and we care more about their attitudes toward us than we do about the attitudes of strangers toward us.

Consequences of friendship are always a contingent matter, i.e. it is never a necessary truth that a particular friendship will have certain consequences. If, however, friendship is intrinsically valuable, then it will be a necessary truth that friendship will add value to one's life because that intrinsic value would be a matter of friendship's essential nature, not merely of its contingent consequences. Does friendship have intrinsic value? An answer to this question will have to wait upon our examination of friendship and of intrinsic value in the following chapters.

1.3 FRIENDSHIP AND MORALITY

In ordinary discourse, we often contrast what is good or best for the individual with what morality requires of her. We can think of cases in which it seems obvious that doing what morality requires is not compatible with the agent doing what is best for herself. For example, imagine that you are living in Nazi Germany and you are friendly with the family living next door to you. This family, however, is Jewish, and so is in extreme danger. It seems that morality requires you to aid this family in hiding from or evading the Nazis, but in so doing you would put yourself in grave danger. Given that the Nazis will imprison and torture, perhaps even kill you if you are caught, it would seem that what is best for you is to leave your neighbors to fend for themselves and just keep your head down. This latter course of action gives you the best chances of surviving the war without being sent to a concentration camp or being tortured by the Gestapo.

There are philosophers who have challenged this picture of there being any sort of conflict or even potential conflict between the demands of morality or virtue and the demands of self-interest. In the *Republic*, Glaucon famously challenges Socrates to show that we have any reasons to be moral if we can get away with immorality and thereby promote our own good. Socrates purports to show Glaucon that an immoral life is always worse for the agent than is a moral or virtuous life. Similarly, in his *Nichomachean Ethics*, Aristotle argues that the best life for a human being is a life lived in accordance with virtue.

Thomas Hobbes, and contemporary philosophers such as David Gauthier working in the Hobbesian vein, take a very different approach to reconciling the demands of morality and the demands of self-interest.[9] Hobbes took reasons of self-interest as fundamental but showed how everyone acting independently to promote his or her own good creates a situation in which we all end up leading lives that are "solitary, poor, nasty, brutish, and short."[10] So, Hobbes argues, we need to put in place a powerful sovereign who enforces laws that require behavior that mimics that required by the conventional rules of morality. Thus, once we are out of the state of nature and in the commonwealth, acting 'morally' is in our best interests, and it is in our best interests to get out of the state of nature and into the commonwealth.

These issues about the connection or divide between self-interest and morality arise at several points in relation to friendship. We have to ask ourselves with respect to any particular person, "Should I become friends with her?" Often we take the answer to this question to depend upon how we think that a relationship with, say, Isabel, would make our lives go better. Are we going to enjoy spending time with Isabel? Are we going to be able to talk openly with Isabel and thereby take comfort and support from her? Will Isabel mix well with our other friends? Will Isabel be overly demanding and needy? But there is another question, one that rarely occurs to us as we deliberate about whether to make Isabel our friend: am I morally permitted to become friends with Isabel?

This question is likely to sound odd to many people: how or why would morality forbid me to make a friend? There are several possible answers to this question, the first four dealing with the possible consequences of a given friendship and the last having to do with someone's meriting or deserving friendship.

First, suppose that Isabel is a morally bad person: she is petty, greedy, concerned only with superficial matters such as status and appearance, is willing to tear others down in order to build herself up, and helps others only to the extent that she thinks that she can gain by doing so. If I spend time with Isabel, there is a chance that I will be influenced by her and thereby become more like her than I might already be. In other words, a friendship with Isabel has the potential to corrupt and degrade me, thereby undermining my own moral decency. It is plausible to suppose that morality forbids me from doing what would lead to my own moral corruption, so it is plausible to suppose that morality forbids me from befriending Isabel in such a case.

Second, again supposing that Isabel is a morally bad person, my becoming friends with Isabel will make it the case that I have reasons to promote Isabel's good. In fact, many, if not most philosophers of friendship believe that we have special obligations to promote the good of our friends, to be partial to them. If Isabel were my friend, then, I would be obligated to give her a kind of preferential treatment, to promote her good before I promote the good of strangers or of mere acquaintances. Given Isabel's character, I would be promoting the well-being of a bad person, thereby allowing her to devote more time and effort to her morally vicious projects and goals.[11] Surely morality forbids me from engaging in activities that lead me to promote wrong-doing, so it thereby forbids my befriending Isabel.

Third, no matter what Isabel's character, my special obligations to her if she were my friend would make it the case that I have fewer resources to devote to fulfilling my impartial duties to promote the well-being of other animals and humans, no matter what their relationship to me. Thus, there will be times at which I will be obligated to promote Isabel's well-being even though there are other persons and animals in greater, perhaps even far greater need than Isabel is. So the demands of impartial morality might dictate that I not make friends with Isabel because, by doing so, I would decrease (and in fact be morally obligated to decrease) the contributions that I would be able to make to overall well-being.

Fourth, becoming friends with Isabel will detract from the amount of time and other resources that I have to devote to those who are already my friends, and to my other loved ones such as family members. The more friends that I have, the more difficult it becomes to fulfill my special obligations to each of them. Thus, before I make a new friend, I need to think about all of my present commitments and obligations, partial or impartial, and consider whether I can realistically balance the commitments and demands that would arise from a new friendship.

And finally, fifth, some philosophers regard friendship and love as responses to other persons that can be either warranted or unwarranted by the character of that other. If Isabel is a morally bad person, then, such philosophers might insist that

Isabel is not deserving of my friendship because she is not worthy of being loved. Thus, in such a case, I morally ought to refrain from befriending Isabel in favor of finding a morally decent person who is worthy of love and friendship.[12]

On the other hand, there are some reasons why it might be thought that morality gives me reason to make a particular friend, say, Isabel.

First, one might think that the best way to promote overall welfare is to get to know some people very well. Then, we will be in the position of being able to promote their well-being much better than if we had not become friends with them: we will know what they need and what will best promote their interests. There are some goods that people will not accept unless it is a friend or other loved one providing it, and so if I become friends with Isabel I can provide her with goods that she may not otherwise get.[13]

Second, I cannot fulfill any of my obligations or do any good if I am not at least minimally well-off. If friends will provide me with comfort, support, and pleasure, then I will be better able to devote my efforts to making sacrifices for the greater good. I will have the confidence and support needed to formulate long-term plans and put forth the effort and commitment necessary to see them through. So friends can help us to do more good in the world than if we were lonely and unsupported by loved ones – after all, most of us are just not like Charlie the CDC team leader that I discussed earlier.

Third, if Isabel is a bad person, maybe she will make me worse, as we discussed previously. But maybe I can make her better. By befriending Isabel, I can get to know her better, learn how best to influence and persuade her, and set an example to guide her toward a more virtuous life. Similarly, if I have moral flaws, I can seek out and befriend people who can help to make me morally better. Sometimes, we strive to be better if we believe that doing so will please a loved one and make her proud of us, and so befriending the virtuous Isabel might be dictated by a moral concern that I become a better person.

Fourth, some philosophers follow Aristotle in viewing friendship as an arena for the exercise of virtues. If Isabel and I are both devoted to the promotion of good, we can sustain and aid each other in carrying out that commitment. But also, if caring for others and exhibiting loving behavior are themselves virtuous, then we need to have friends or other loved ones for whom we can care and toward whom we can act in a loving manner. And it may be that friends allow us to exhibit a kind of care and love that we cannot exhibit in, for example, loving relationships with parents or children – friends are more often on an equal footing than are parents and children, and are often drawn together by common interests rather than by familial bonds, and so relationships between friends can call forth different kinds of loving care.

And again fifth and finally, Isabel might be someone who deserves my love and devotion. Just as very bad people may not be worthy or deserving of being loved, some philosophers insist, so good people deserve to be loved. If morality places a duty upon us to ensure that people are treated in accordance with their merit, then morality requires each of us to seek out and to befriend those worthy of our friendship (or, at least, to seek them out and ensure that they find compatible friends, if we are not such ourselves).

Let us suppose that I befriended Isabel after deciding that morality either required or permitted me to do so. Once Isabel and I are friends, I need to determine what, if anything, I now owe Isabel in virtue of her being my friend. As I have said, many philosophers of friendship agree that we have special obligations to care for our friends, although they disagree about the grounds and nature of those obligations. Not only do I, then, have to determine the content of my special obligations to Isabel, I also have to try to figure out (i) how to balance those obligations against my other moral obligations, and (ii) how to balance those obligations against my reasons to promote my own interests. We might enter some friendship believing that it will make our lives go better, but if circumstances – or we or our friend – change, it might be that the moral demands of the friendship require uncompensated sacrifice from us.

As we explore the connections between living a good life and friendship, then, we have to be aware that there are at least two other, intersecting questions. Does friendship impact our moral characters? What is the connection between our moral characters and our living a good life?

The role that friendship plays in our moral characters is an important one as technologies change. If it is true that technology allows us to make friendships quicker and to make more of them, we may be less attuned to the characters of our friends and to the impact that our interactions with them have on our own characters. Depending on the role that our characters have on our ability to live a good life, we may then also be less attuned to how our friendships are impacting the quality of our lives.

1.4 VALUE, HAPPINESS, AND WELFARE

Before we move on to a discussion of the nature of friendship in Chapter Two, I need to say a few words about the concept of the good life. An important focus of this book is the connection between friendship and the good life (and thus of how technology, in impacting our friendships, is impacting the quality of our lives). How do our friendships affect or connect to our leading good lives? In evaluating how, say, Isabel's life is going, there are several different questions we might ask. Is Isabel doing well? Is Isabel happy? Is Isabel leading a good life? Is Isabel leading a valuable life? We need to have some idea of how these questions are related to one another if we are to address our fundamental question about the connection between friendship and the good life.

Let us begin with the concept of happiness. For many people, happiness has a subjective connotation.[14] In other words, when we describe someone as 'happy' or say that a person is 'leading a happy life,' we are saying something about the way that her life feels to her from the inside. A happy person is enjoying her life and she feels contented. Whether a happy person is living a valuable life is, then, a function of how we understand value. If an intrinsically valuable life is one in which pleasure predominates over pain, then it would seem that a happy person is living a valuable life, and someone living a valuable life is, at least more often than not, happy. If, however, we think that an intrinsically valuable life is determined by something other than how the agent feels from the inside, then a happy person may not be living a valuable life, and a person living a valuable life may not be happy.

I will be focusing on the concept of a valuable life: what must a person's life be like for her life to be intrinsically valuable? Some concepts of what makes a life valuable, such as the Hedonist view which holds that all and only pleasure is intrinsically valuable, will also look like lives that most people would deem happy. But other concepts of a valuable life – for example, concepts that put moral virtue at the center of such a life – might look, at least in some cases, like unhappy lives: think of the person who is tortured and dies as a result of helping her Jewish neighbors hide from the Nazis. Some philosophers will find it plausible to suppose that, whatever a good life is, it must also be a life that it seems reasonable to call happy, but others will disagree. So, as we consider whether our friends contribute to the value of our lives, we can also consider whether, in doing so, they make us happy, always recognizing that our answers to these questions may very well come apart.

I think that it is quite clear that if we are asking whether an individual is doing well, we do not want to be thinking about whether her life is instrumentally valuable. Consider an example: Ted is a heroin addict. His addiction leads him to a life on the streets where he scrounges and begs for food, and resorts to theft in order to get his fix of heroin. Ted dies of an overdose at the age of 23. Suppose that Tina, a documentary filmmaker, films Ted's last years and then shows her film as part of a drug awareness program for at-risk youths. If many young people who would otherwise have resorted to drugs take Ted's example to heart and instead lead long, productive lives, then Ted's miserable life had great instrumental value: his suffering and early death had very good consequences. But I do not think anyone would want to say that Ted led a good life: it is the intrinsic badness of his life as a heroin addict that allowed him, as portrayed by Tina, to have such a good effect on a lot of young people.[15]

Finally, we have to be careful when we use the expression 'good life.' This term is ambiguous between 'intrinsically valuable life' and 'morally virtuous life.' As I pointed out in the previous section, there are interesting questions about the connection between welfare or the good life and morality or virtue, and there are also interesting questions about whether moral action or virtue is good for its own sake or as an end. For just these reasons, we want to avoid begging any questions by equating a morally good life with a valuable life. So when I use 'good,' I will mean 'intrinsically valuable,' not 'morally good.' In asking about the connection between friendship and the good life, we are asking about the connection between friendship and a life good for its own sake (intrinsically valuable). Whether that life involves virtue is a further and different question.

Now that we have a clear idea of the questions that we are trying to answer, we can start by considering what a friendship is.

NOTES

1 In *Nichomachean Ethics*, translated by Terence Irwin (Indianapolis, IN: Hackett Publishing, 1985): 1155a5.

2 Let us simply assume that one can access the internet even if one chooses to have one's friend physically accompany one. Thus, in choosing that physical company, one will not forego contact with life back on Earth.

3 Hayley Tsukayana, "Your Facebook friends have more friends than you do," *The Washington Post*, February 3, 2012 (www.washingtonpost.com/business/technology/your-facebook-friends-have-more-friends-than-you/2012/02/03/gIQAuNUlmQ_story.html?noredirect=on&utm_term=.9f5b6887ba57).

4 Dean Cocking and Steve Matthews, "Unreal Friends," *Ethics and Information Technology* 2 (2000), 223–231: 224.

5 Post-Kripke and Putnam these issues have become much more controversial. On one way of thinking of it, Kripke has brought back the notion of something like an essential property: things like fire, water, and metal have essential properties that are not part of their definition but without which they could not exist. All of this is very complicated and I certainly cannot explore the details of Kripke's metaphysics and philosophy of language here. See Saul Kripke, *Naming and Necessity* (Cambridge, MA: Harvard University Press, 1980).

6 The astute reader has probably noticed that in talking about conceivability I have talked about what *can* and *cannot* be conceived. Of course, these are precisely the concepts which we are trying to understand. Trying

to remove this circularity is no easy task, and thus we should take the conceivability 'test' as a heuristic that gives the novice a feel for the strength of the concept with which we are working.

7 Not all philosophers agree with Plato on this point. For example, Kant would say that pleasure is only good as an end if it is the pleasure of a virtuous person. In fact, Plato himself says that *harmless* pleasures are good for their own sake, suggesting, perhaps, that malicious pleasures (pleasures derived from the suffering of others) are not good for their own sake. See Plato, *Republic*, translated by Desmond Lee (New York, NY: Penguin Books, 1974): 357b, and Immanuel Kant, *Grounding for the Metaphysics of Morals*, translated by James W. Ellington (Indianapolis, IN: Hackett Publishing, 1993): 393.

8 However, some situation involving pleasure might, on balance, be bad, even if the pleasure itself is good. If Johnny gets pleasure from torturing kittens and puppies, the situation in which he does so might very well be overall bad because the pain of the kittens and puppies outweighs the pleasure that Johnny takes in torturing them.

9 Thomas Hobbes, *Leviathan*, edited by Edwin Curley (Indianapolis, IN: Hackett Publishing, 1994), and David Gauthier, *Morals by Agreement* (Oxford: Oxford University Press, 1986).

10 *Leviathan*: 76.

11 This is unless Isabel's well-being requires the improvement of her moral character. Then, my caring for Isabel will involve aiding her in becoming morally better. This issue will be discussed further in the coming chapters.

12 For a summary of the range of views that philosophers have taken with respect to whether love requires justification or depends upon an evaluation of the beloved, see Bennett Helm, "Love," *Stanford Encyclopedia of Philosophy* (https://plato.stanford.edu/entries/love/#LoveValu).

13 Of course, morality might then demand that I befriend Isabel even if I would rather befriend Misha. But Misha might be in high demand as a friend, given his charm and kindness, while Isabel's shyness and awkwardness renders her less attractive as a friend. So Isabel is less likely to get the goods that one can only get from friends, and so it seems that I ought to befriend Isabel to ensure that she will get those goods. Misha, after all, is likely to have plenty of people from whom he can receive such goods.

14 However, see Richard Kraut, "Two Conceptions of Happiness," *Philosophical Review* 88 (1979), 167–197. See also Fred Feldman, *What is This Thing Called Happiness?* (Oxford: Oxford University Press, 2010) for an extensive analysis of the concept of happiness.

15 We will see in Chapter Four that this actually depends upon whether Ted wanted his life to serve as a warning for at-risk young people. If that is what Ted wanted most, then, at least on some conceptions of a good life, Ted in fact led an intrinsically valuable life.

Two

In recent years, we have seen what are, supposedly, new incarnations of the friendship relation. Perhaps most importantly, people now describe some others as their 'Facebook friends.' If Sara and Emma both have Facebook pages, Sara can send Emma a 'friend request.' If Emma accepts that request, she thereby allows Sara to view what she, Emma, has posted on her page and also to post comments on that page. At any time, Emma can 'defriend' Sara, thereby blocking Sara from any further access to Emma's page. In some ways, Facebook friends are the modern, technologically advanced form of what used to be called 'pen pals': pen pals often had never met each other in person, but they would communicate about their lives through physical letters sent through the postal service and might also include photographs enclosed with those letters. However, pen pals would each craft their communications with the other person specifically in mind. On Facebook, on the other hand, postings are usually available to any number of the hundred-or-so 'friends' that the average person has. Also, unlike with pen pals, many people have met most of their Facebook friends in person at some point in time (but they usually have not met them all).

The prevalence of reality TV, with a large tween and teenage audience, has led to the coining of the term 'frenemy,' formed from combining 'friend' and 'enemy.' Friendships between young people are often characterized by dramatic conflict mirroring the dramatic changes and conflicts within the self at that time of life. In such relationships, those who are supposedly one's friends, then, often interact with one in confrontational and argumentative ways, ways that are more standardly associated with interactions between 'enemies.' Of course, such relationships are not limited to young people, as the bickering-laden and drama-fueled relationships on shows such as *Real Housewives of [various large US cities]* and *Dance Moms* demonstrate.

In this chapter, I am going to explore the nature of friendship by examining various features of an interpersonal relationship that have been regarded by philosophers as being the distinctive or essential feature of a friendship. I think that it is important to consider each of these features, although in the end, I argue, no one of them is the distinguishing characteristic of friendship. Friendship, I argue, is a relationship of intimacy, where the precise nature of that intimacy will vary from one friendship to another. Intimacy involves some cluster of those features discussed by philosophers of friendship, but combined in different ways and in varying strengths in individual relationships. Friendship is a highly complex phenomenon, and this complexity is important to keep in mind as, in later chapters, we consider how technology affects friendship and how friendship contributes to living a good life.

I will use frenemies as a running example as I consider each of the various features of friendship. One of the reasons why the term was created by combining 'friend' with 'enemy' is that what have come to be known as frenemies are individuals who appear to have a relationship that is conflicted in various ways: they sometimes act in ways characteristic of friends, at other times they act in ways that seem incompatible with genuine friendship. Seeing how such conflicted relationships can yet be considered, in at least some cases, to be genuine friendships can, then, help to illuminate just how complex our concept and the reality of friendship really is.

Frenemies also allow us an opportunity to examine the role of morality and virtue in friendship. The behavior of frenemies with respect to one another often appears petty, hypocritical, backstabbing, and generally reprehensible. In other words, frenemies appear to often treat each other in ways that no one would label virtuous or morally commendable. Thus, their behavior casts doubt on their moral characters in at least certain respects. Aristotle famously argued that genuine friends must at least meet some minimum standard of virtue, while Laurence Thomas has more recently argued that an important function of friendship in human life is the mutual promotion of moral commitment. Consideration of frenemies thus allows us to explore the plausibility of such 'moralized' accounts of friendship.[1] This is particularly important since, as I pointed out in Chapter One, philosophers have debated about the role of virtue and morality in the living of a good life. Thus, friendship's relationship to morality is relevant to its relationship to the good life.

As we look at the various features of friendship, we need to keep in mind our responses to the thought experiment with which I began Chapter One: in this thought experiment, you are to imagine yourself moving to a different planet. Responses to the case would seem to indicate that we prefer the company of friends to long-term solitude and that we prefer the physical presence of friends to their virtual presence of one form or another. As we consider the features of friendship in this chapter, we will consider what lies behind our first response of desiring to have friends to alleviate long-term solitude. In the next chapter, we will consider the importance of embodiment to friendship as we examine the role of social media, and Facebook in particular, in friendship. We will then be in a position, in Chapter Four, to connect friendship to the good life for human beings.

So let us consider the features that have most often been regarded as distinctive or characteristic of the friendship relationship: mutual special concern (covered in section 2.1), special knowledge of each other (section 2.2), distinctive forms of responsiveness and/or interaction (section 2.3), and love, or something akin to love (section 2.4).

2.1 CARING FOR ANOTHER FOR HER OWN SAKE

Darren starts asking Samantha to have lunch or tea with him, to accompany him to movies and parties, and generally just to hang out together. In other words, Darren engages in the sort of behavior that is characteristic of attempts to befriend someone. Samantha eagerly accepts all of Darren's invitations, glad to be his plus-one at parties, his dinner companion, and to hang out with him. After a couple of years, others think of Darren and Samantha as friends and they think of each other in that way. We can also suppose that Darren and Samantha feel and exhibit concern for each other's well-being. Are Darren and Samantha friends?

Our initial inclination to say 'yes' to this question might be weakened by various possible accounts of the basis of the concern that Darren and Samantha have for each other. Suppose that Darren cares about Samantha because she holds a very prominent position in the profession in which he is hoping to advance, and he believes that by 'befriending' her he will be able to exert influence over her so that she will use her connections and reputation to advance his career. Samantha accepts Darren's invitations because Darren is very charming and handsome, and she believes that having him as her escort or companion at various events will enhance her social capital and make some of her frenemies jealous. She cares about Darren, then, because she wants him to be available to serve her social purposes, just as he cares about her in virtue of her ability to advance his career. Given these facts about the bases of their concern for each other, it is likely that Darren will cease to care about Samantha if she loses her professional reputation, and Samantha will cease to care about Darren if he suffers an accident which mars his good looks and causes him to be constantly depressed and angry.

Aristotle famously called relationships such as that between Darren and Samantha 'friendships for advantage.'[2] In such relationships, the parties care about each other only instrumentally: they care about each other only as means to various benefits that they can get from one another, benefits such as professional and social advancement.[3] Another familiar form of such a relationship is one in which one or both of the parties 'uses' the other only in order to gain sexual pleasure.[4] We can certainly imagine Darren saying to Samantha in such a case, "You never really cared about me! You only cared about the sex!" It seems that Samantha is using Darren only as a tool to her own ends, and fails to care about Darren for his own sake, where caring about someone for his own sake is to care about him *simpliciter*, not merely as a means to achieve some of one's goals. Aristotle insisted that in genuine friendships (what he called 'complete' friendships) the parties care about each other for their own sake.

But what exactly is involved in caring about another person for her own sake? It is often the case that we are led to befriend another person because we enjoy her company and find solace and comfort in her presence. Suppose that Jerry and Elaine have been friends because they appreciate each other's sense of humor: they can make each other laugh even in the darkest of times. But Jerry now becomes involved in various political causes to such an extent that his seriousness suppresses his previous willingness to engage humor about even the most serious of events. He now chastises Elaine for what he regards as her frivolity, insisting that they must focus on the terrible plight of much of the world's population. Elaine no longer enjoys Jerry's company: rather than offering her joy and comfort, he makes her feel depressed, guilty, and inadequate. So she ceases to spend time with Jerry, effectively ending their friendship.

Did Elaine care about Jerry for his own sake? One reason that might lead us to answer 'no' is that Elaine failed to maintain her friendship with Jerry in spite of the various changes that he has undergone. If she really cared about him as a person, rather than only as a means to her own enjoyment and comfort, then wouldn't she continue to care about him even if he no longer offers her pleasure and comfort? After all, it might be said, Jerry is still the same person even though his interests and personality have changed. So if Elaine cared about him for his own sake, she would continue to care about him and to be his friend in spite of the changes that he has undergone.

However, this view of what it is to care about another for her own sake is highly implausible or, at least, highly unattractive as an account of how we ought to care about our friends. Suppose that the political causes to which Jerry has become dedicated are neo-Nazism and other hate movements, causes which Elaine finds odious and morally repugnant. (For simplicity's sake, there is no possibility of Elaine's being able to talk Jerry out of his new commitments.) So now not only does she no longer find joy and comfort in Jerry's company, she also regards his commitments as morally heinous. What is there left for her to care about as regards Jerry? Some bare essence, soul, or Cartesian ego? Surely that is not the sort of thing about which any of us can actually care.[5] Supposing that friends must care about each other for each other's own sake is an unattractive ideal if doing so requires that the friends care about each other in spite of whatever drastic changes they might undergo.

Aristotle regarded the best sort of friendship as lasting. So if friends are to care about each other for their own sake and that care is to endure, then, according to Aristotle, friends must be virtuous persons.[6] Aristotelian 'complete' friends care about each other because of their virtuous character – each cares about the other for the virtuous person she is – and because, according to Aristotle, virtue is enduring, so will complete friendship be enduring. Virtuous people do not become neo-Nazis, so Jerry was never Elaine's genuine friend, according to Aristotle. If Jerry and Elaine were complete friends, then they would be virtuous, their virtue would endure, and so the basis of their concern for each other would endure: all other changes that they might undergo would be irrelevant to the bases of their concern for each other.

Most of us, however, can give plenty of examples of people who we do not regard as virtuous and yet do regard as having been friends: Bonnie and Clyde, Thelma and Louise, and Butch Cassidy and the Sundance Kid. Once we reject caring about someone through whatever changes she might undergo as the sort of care present in friendship, what conception of caring about someone for her own sake can we put in its place?

Let us contrast the initial case of Jerry and Elaine with the previous ones I gave in which (i) Darren cared about Samantha only as a means to career advancement, and Samantha cared about Darren only as a source of social capital, and (ii) Darren and Samantha cared about each other only as a means to sexual gratification. Jerry and Elaine cared about each other in virtue of the other's sense of humor and ability to offer comfort in difficult times. Now imagine that each of Jerry and Elaine sees his or her sense of humor and ability to comfort as a central positive trait of his or her character, and so welcomes the other's appreciation of it. In a case such as (ii), people often feel demeaned if they are valued only for their sexuality: they say that the other does not see them as a person but only as a body. So if you find yourself in such a relationship, you might feel that you are cared about, as Neal Delaney puts it, "for things about you that don't strike you as important to who you are or what you're about."[7] It seems that we want to be cared about in virtue of qualities that we ourselves regard as somehow central to our identity: we want to be loved not just for what we are but for what we take to be important or significant about ourselves (or, perhaps, for what we *would* take to be significant about ourselves if we had relevant and sufficient self-knowledge). And, in fact, this may not be compatible with being cared about through any and all changes: many people would react with disgust if their partner, for example, told them that he or she would still care about them even if they became a neo-Nazi as long as they remained sexually appealing and good in bed.

I think that we also want to make a distinction between caring about someone in virtue of their personality or character traits and loving them only in virtue of how those traits impact us. Suppose that Jerry is an undocumented immigrant who is apprehended and deported. He and Elaine are no longer able to see or to keep in contact with each other. If Jerry and Elaine have the sort of concern for each other that we expect friends to have, then each will continue to want the other to be doing well, to be happy, even if the other's happiness has no causal effects on their own lives. If Elaine were to say, "I don't care anymore about what becomes of Jerry. After all, what does that have to do with me anymore?", I am confident that most of us would be appalled and would wonder if Elaine ever genuinely cared about Jerry rather than just about how Jerry could make her feel.[8]

Although it seems right to say, as Aristotle did, that friends care about each other for the other's own sake, it turns out, then, not to be a simple matter to say what such concern amounts to. But we might think that, whatever it comes to, it is not present in the relationship between frenemies. Frenemies exhibit jealousy over each other's successes, bicker and fight about supposed betrayals and transgressions, and complain about each other to third parties. High drama is a common feature of frenemy relationships. However, these periods of conflict and animosity are interspersed with times in which the parties support each other – now complaining about the betrayals and transgressions of those third parties – and take pleasure in each other's company. Frenemies certainly seem to have a need for each other, but need is compatible with a purely instrumental concern: we may need other people to act as our 'punching bags,' as it were, but that need is compatible with a lack of genuine concern. Is it plausible to suppose that people who care about each other for each other's own sake would act in the ways that frenemies do?

Once we allow that less-than-virtuous people can exhibit the sort of care for each other appropriate to friendship, I think that we should allow that the behavior of frenemies can be compatible with that appropriate sort of concern. Let us imagine a stereotypical instance of frenemies. Jenny and Louise are both realtors in the same town. They often have lunch or drinks together and get together for movies, barbecues, and other events. It is, however, common for Jenny and Louise to gripe to third parties about the behavior of the other, saying that she, for example, stole her customers, lied about her to customers in order to lure them away, or undermined her in some other way. They will make nasty remarks about each other's photos in their advertisements and complain about each other in a multitude of other ways.

Much, I think, depends on why Jenny and Louise interact in the ways that they do. One common reason for such behavior is a sense of insecurity: it is not unusual for people to attempt to build themselves up by knocking each other down. Friends can provide a handy source of ego-building and of ego-deflating: we often share interests and undertakings in common with our friends, so their successes and failures are easily comparable to our own. Perhaps in order to handle our own failures, highlighted by a friend's successes, we need to claw at them behind their backs. Only by acting in such a way can we continue to interact with the other and support her without having our own sense of self-worth undermined.

But shouldn't people who care about each other want the best for each other, regardless of what light that puts them in? Shouldn't they be engaged in mutual support of each other's sense of self-worth rather than needing to pick at each other in order to build themselves up? Shouldn't they always be trying to see each other in the best light possible? The answer to all of these questions is of course 'yes,' but people do not always act and feel as they ought to act and feel. Our own insecurities can cause us to act in uncharitable ways to people about whom we genuinely care. We need to be sure not to confuse caring about someone for her own sake and behaving as we ought to behave toward those about whom we so care. In fact, we might think that frenemy-ish behavior is indicative of a trust in the care of the other: we can bicker and pick at each other, thereby venting insecurities and frustrations, without fear of alienating each other. (This sort of behavior is common between siblings.) Much depends on whether Jenny and Louise, for example, are willing to put aside this behavior in times of great need on the part of the other, say in the case of illness or the loss of a loved one. We must not confuse Jenny's failure to act as a friend ought to act with respect to Louise, and Jenny's not actually being friends with Louise. Accusing someone of not acting as a friend ought to act is compatible with, and in fact depends for its accusative force upon, the background assumption that that person is actually one's friend.

What I am suggesting is that, as demonstrated by an illustrative case of frenemies, a wide range of behavior is compatible with genuine concern. Thus, a wide range of behaviors is compatible with friendship, even given that friendship requires non-instrumental concern. Further, even though we care about our friends, we also care about ourselves. The fact that frenemies often appear narcissistic and self-centered does not undermine the status of their relationship as a friendship: it perhaps demonstrates instead too much love of self, a love of self that too often outweighs one's concern for one's friend.

2.2 SELF-REVELATION AND FRIENDSHIP

Although I have set aside Aristotle's requirement that genuine friends must be virtuous (to at least some degree), the requirement did allow Aristotle to explain a common feature of friendships: friends usually trust one another. He says that two people can only love each other for the other's own sake if they have "time to grow accustomed to each other" so they can grasp how the other's character exhibits virtue.[9] Once Tony and Roger know each other, they can recognize each other's virtue and they will then trust each other, because each believes that the other is virtuous and knows that the virtuous do not engage in serious wrong-doing. If Elaine loves Jerry in virtue of his ability to make her laugh, Elaine, according to Aristotle, has no reason to trust Jerry: having a good sense of humor is entirely compatible with being treacherous and cruel. Thus, unlike in the case of Tony and Roger, if Elaine is told that Jerry has done a terrible wrong, she has no reason not to believe the report, even if the report concerns a betrayal of herself by Jerry.

But trust may be secured by means other than mutual recognition of virtuous character. Laurence Thomas has argued that the "enormous bond of mutual trust" that exists between friends is "cemented by equal self-disclosure, and, for that very reason, is a sign of the very special regard which each [friend] has for the other."[10] Here Thomas is pointing to another feature of a relationship that we often regard as an element of friendship: mutual self-disclosure, and thus mutual special knowledge. Our friends are people we know, not just in the sense of being acquainted with them but in the sense of having knowledge and understanding of them that others do not have, or, at least, that only some others have. But what sort of knowledge and understanding do friends have of one another and how do they acquire such knowledge?

I think that the form and content of self-disclosure will vary from one friendship to another. Some friends spend a great deal of time together just talking, while others do not. In the latter sort of case, sometimes self-disclosure is very gradual as small snippets of self-revelation drop between holes on the golf course, and sometimes it occurs primarily in a non-verbal way. For most people, 'how they are' when with friends is quite different from 'how they are' when with mere acquaintances or strangers, and the kind of behavior we display around friends can be quite revealing. For example, there are some jokes that I will tell a friend but no one else, and I will try to suppress the expression of certain emotions around strangers but not around friends. So self-disclosure will not always be verbal and the knowledge that we have of our friends may be experiential, as it were: we know what it is like to laugh at private jokes with one another, we know what it is like to be comforted by each other, etc.

Just as the way in which friends reveal themselves to each other will vary from one friendship to another, so will the content of the revelations. We rarely tell any one person everything about ourselves. For example, Samantha may tell her husband Darren almost everything, but not about the fact that she finds herself attracted to Larry: this fact she reveals only to Serena as she tries to work through her guilt about this attraction. This does not show that she does not trust or respect Darren. Rather, we can trust different people with different aspects of ourselves. So if Laura has rather kinky sexual fantasies, she may feel comfortable telling Sally because she knows that Sally is uninhibited, but she will not tell Rob because Rob had a very strict Catholic upbringing and would be shocked by Laura's fantasies. Each friend that we have will know us in a different sort of way: they will know different aspects of ourselves, and the way in which they have come to possess that knowledge will differ.

The nature of a friendship can often be grasped by an understanding not only of what friends have actually revealed to one another but also of what those friends *expect* to have revealed to them by the other. Consider the following example: Sam is undergoing treatment for a serious illness. He does not tell either of his friends, Dean and Cassie, that he is ill and in need of such treatment because he does not want to worry them or make them feel obligated to offer him help and support, nor does he want them to see him in a weak and dependent condition. Only when the treatment is over and he has recovered does he tell both Dean and Cassie about what he has been through. Suppose that Dean is hurt and upset that Sam did not tell him, while Cassie is not — she just says that she is glad that Sam is better and to let her know if he needs any assistance during his continuing recovery.

Dean's reaction reveals that he has an understanding of his friendship with Sam that involves showing needs and asking for and receiving help. Cassie's friendship with Sam is different: they care about each other but also are willing to allow the other to put up boundaries around parts of themselves that they judge less than admirable or attractive for one reason or other. Different friendships are not only based on different revelations about ourselves but also *demand* different revelations of us. Dean may well be justified in being angry and upset with Sam, while it would be inappropriate for Cassie to react in the same way.

We do not want to assess friendships by the sheer amount of information that the parties to the relationship have about one another. Tony may know a multitude of facts about Roger: that he is lazy about flossing, that he never wears socks to bed, that he has an ingrown toenail, that he has three different kinds of sticky notes on his desk, etc. But the knowledge characteristic of friends is knowledge garnered through interaction, and it is knowledge that somehow allows one to have an understanding of at least some aspects of the other's character. Tony may have lots of bits of information about Roger, but may yet be unable to put those bits together to form any kind of revealing picture of who Roger is as a person. Of course, different friends will have different pictures of Roger as a person because they will have interacted with him in different kinds of ways and his revelations to them will have been in response to their revelations to him about themselves. As I pointed out previously, we reveal different aspects of ourselves to different persons, and an important reason for this is that different people call forth different aspects of us. Further, the nature of our history of interaction with each friend is different, and commonalities in our pasts can allow us interpretations of current attitudes and behaviors of our friends that persons without that history of interaction could never achieve. My friend Tracy and I went to graduate school together, and that experience allows us to understand various intentional and non-intentional revelations to one another in ways that no one else can.

How do frenemies fare with respect to mutual self-disclosure? Much of the character of the relationship between frenemies is a result of the parties to the relationship having disclosed themselves to each other in various kinds of ways. Frenemies, such as our previous case of Jenny and Louise, often bicker, snipe at each other, complain about each other to other people, use confidences to undermine each other, etc. Part of what allows frenemies to wield such power over each other is precisely the fact that they have a knowledge and understanding of each other that goes beyond the norm. They know each other's insecurities and vulnerabilities, and this is what allows them to make each other so angry and resentful.

Given that frenemies often have a unique and distinctive perspective on each other, and that their relationship is yet characterized by periods of resentment, jealousy, and even animosity, I think shows that mutual self-disclosure does not guarantee trust and is not necessarily a sign of regard, as Thomas would have it be. Knowing another person well can be a source of distrust and suspicion. Of course, Thomas and Aristotle would both say that in such an instance the mutual self-disclosure is not sufficient for friendship. I agree that such self-disclosure needs to occur in a particular sort of context, as I will discuss further later. However, I have already suggested that frenemies can be genuinely concerned about one another, so part of that context seems already in place, at least in some frenemy-ships.

2.3 SPENDING TIME WITH OUR FRIENDS

2.3.1 Showing concern for each other

It is characteristic of friends that they want to spend time with one another, be together, and engage in various sorts of activities – playing tennis, going to the movies, attending a book club, having dinner – with one another. And, in fact, it seems that for a friendship to exist the parties must have interacted with one another somehow, and that that interaction must, in some way, have exhibited the concern that they have for each other.

In their influential article "Friendship and the Self,"[11] Dean Cocking and Jeanette Kennett offer a particular account of this kind of concerned interaction, focusing on the way in which interaction between friends shapes their choices, interests, and even their conceptions of themselves. As they say, "in friendship, I am distinctively receptive both to the other's interests and to their way of seeing me ... [thus,] the self my friend sees is, at least in part, a product of the friendship."[12] Friendship, according to Cocking and Kennett, changes the parties to it and those changes then shape the continuing interactions between the friends.

Let's consider a case in order to see what Cocking and Kennett have in mind. Suppose that Jerry and George tell each other everything, every intimate detail of their lives, and they do so because each trusts the other not to betray him and they intend their revelations to be expressions of this trust. This latter fact is reinforced by the fact that each knows that no one else knows as much about the other as he does and that there are certain things that each knows about the other that no one else knows. They can also read each other's body language and can garner knowledge about each other beyond that which is verbally or intentionally related. But importantly, the ways in which George and Jerry understand themselves have been shaped by a responsiveness to the other. So let us suppose that Jerry and George are primarily interested in finding women to date and with whom to have sex. George sees that Jerry picks on little tiny faults of the women he is dating, and George points this out to him, suggesting that Jerry is really looking for ways to avoid long-term commitments. Jerry then starts seeing his criticisms of his dates in a different light. Similarly, Jerry points out that George's lies are not as opaque as he seems to think and, again, George reinterprets his past dating failures. Now George and Jerry are interacting in the way that Cocking and Kennett view as distinctive of friendship: George and Jerry are "characteristically and distinctively receptive to being directed and interpreted and so in these ways drawn by the other."[13]

Although I think that concerned interaction can take a variety of forms, I also think that Cocking and Kennett are pointing to an important feature of many friendships: we come to take seriously that about which our friends care *because* our friends care about that. Perhaps I never had any interest in yoga but my friend Katerina tells me about how her practice has enhanced her life. As her friend, I will be open to hearing what she has to say, and to at least considering trying yoga for myself. But even if I never try yoga, I will find myself being more receptive to understanding why Katerina enjoys and values it. If I was always shut off to interests and concerns of Katerina's that I did not antecedently share, it seems that I am not responding to her in the open way that is characteristic of friendship.

Perhaps most significantly, the caring interaction between friends often involves an openness to each other's interpretation of them. We have revealed ourselves to our friends, both consciously and unconsciously, and friends thus gain a unique understanding of each other. Caring about each other involves paying attention to what the other reveals and then paying attention to what the other says about what we have revealed to her. I may insist that I am not an ambitious person but a friend may very well be in a position to point to behavior that belies my own understanding of myself. We learn about ourselves through our interactions with friends and, in responding to what we learn, we thereby change ourselves in response to how our friends understand us.

Frenemies are an interesting case in terms of our understanding of what caring interaction looks like. There is an important sense in which frenemies do reconstruct their self-understandings in light of each other's view of them, and they also have their interests and concerns shaped by each other. However, the way that this occurs is far from what is most likely envisioned by Cocking and Kennett. In my example of Jerry and George, I imagined each of them helping the other to understand why they have the difficulties in romantic relationships that they do, and each taking the other's evaluation to heart in reforming their perceptions and potentially their actions. But now let's consider Elaine and Sue Ellen, who are frenemies: they tend to read each other's comments in the worst possible light, taking harmless remarks as slights, and they delight in being offended at each other's words and actions. If they shape themselves in response to each other, they do it as a matter of defiance. It seems that if we want to take interpretation and shaping as definitive of friendship, it would be because the interpretation and shaping are ways of showing concern. The way in which frenemies interpret and shape one another is usually not a result of concern, so it does not seem that frenemies are genuine friends.

However, here is where we need to notice that frenemies may come in different forms. Our conception of frenemies as drawn from reality TV tends to be of shallow people who simply delight in tearing others down in order to bolster their own self-images. But we can imagine two people who behave on the surface just as our paradigm frenemies do and yet are genuine friends. Sometimes people who care deeply about one another bicker and quarrel quite often, and this can be a result of being so bound up with one another that they react strongly to any implied criticism or judgment. Some people also just have hot tempers and find that friendship is a place where they can vent and yell and create drama without fear of destroying the relationship (this is often true of relationships between siblings). If Ralph recognizes that Richie needs to blow off steam, then he may, as a perfectly good friend, allow Richie to insult him, to use him as a verbal punching bag. Ralph may then start responding to Richie in kind. Whether or not this is perfectly moral behavior is irrelevant: immature behavior does not disqualify two people from being genuine friends. What is relevant to friendship is the concern expressed in the behavior, not whether it is expressed in the morally appropriate way. It can be true that Ralph and Richie are acting in concerned ways with respect to one another and also that there exist better and perhaps kinder or more productive ways to act on their concern.

2.3.2 Concern and moral character

But can we really interact with people in a way that demonstrates concern if that interaction does not involve attempts to make our friends morally better people? Laurence Thomas would claim that frenemies fail to place friendship in the correct place in their lives, because he understands friendship as having an important role to play in the development and improvement of our moral characters. According to Thomas, friendships are characterized by mutual self-disclosure which leads to trust and is an indication of mutual concern and regard for each other. These features of friendship have important consequences, according to Thomas, for the way in which friends can aid one another to be morally better people.

Friends, through mutual self-disclosure, know each other well: each friend has 'invited' the other "to have a composite moral picture" of her life.[14] My friends know not only that in which I take pride, but also that of which I am ashamed. They know of my moral weaknesses and errors but are able to put these weaknesses into the context of my life as a whole. They understand and love me, and I know this, so I am able to have my moral flaws exposed to them. Given this, friendship provides an open and honest forum for moral self-examination, a space in which we can have our flaws discussed and pointed out without fear of rejection or contempt.

But my friends, given that they care about me, want me to be the best person that I can be, and that includes being the morally best person that I can be. So while they provide a safe space for revelation and examination of my moral flaws, they will not merely accept but will offer criticism in a spirit of love and concern. Given the spirit in which the criticism is offered, it will be easier for me to take it to heart than if it were offered by a stranger or acquaintance: I know my friend loves me and wants the best for me. I also know that her criticism is not an expression of contempt for me but, rather, of the 'special regard' for me that she has, a regard that leads her to want to see my moral improvement.

Similarly, I may be put off by a moral example set by someone who seems too morally saintly or who seems to simply set me in a bad light. My friend's moral example, on the other hand, can be inspiring without being daunting, so friendship will be a space in which each can lead the other to aspire to be better. I want to live up to my friend's best expectations of me, and so will be motivated to take her criticism and her example to heart. While friends as Thomas understands them may not be Aristotelian complete friends, they can inspire each other to aim more fully at virtue and at incorporating goodness into their lives.

Finally, friendship is an arena for the cultivation of moral sensibilities that can be extended to our interactions with persons more generally. Friends "have to be sensitive to deep fears, anxieties, biases, and … a conception of the good life to which the friend subscribes."[15] Thus, friendship helps us to develop empathy and to understand how to engage in moral advising and criticizing with someone over whom we have no authority and who has no authority over us: "[w]hen we proceed ... to grasp the moral experiences of another, especially a companion friend, our moral sensibilities cannot help but be awakened."[16]

Of course, nothing that I have said about what Thomas views as appropriate between friends is true of frenemies. Frenemies do not provide a safe space for moral self-examination and the development of moral sensibilities, because they often use each other's mistakes and weaknesses as ammunition in their petty squabbles. They use their knowledge of each other to better hurt each other when they are involved in quarreling, and they often take pleasure in feeling superior to one another. While frenemies may know each other and genuinely care about each other, their apparent lack of the appropriate sort of 'special regard' for each other undermines trust and thus makes it highly unlikely that their relationship will serve as a forum for moral betterment. Thomas would view frenemies as failing to form the kinds of friendships that can play an important role in helping us to live as the morally best people that we can be.

Thomas would then, I think, say that even if frenemies are genuine friends, they do not act as friends ought to act with respect to one another. If Thomas is correct in thinking that being moral is part of what it is to live a good life, then friends, if they genuinely desire to promote each other's well-being, should act in a way that aims at their mutual moral betterment. Frenemies, then, if they are genuine friends, would be failing with respect to each other because they ought to be acting so as to encourage each other to be morally better: in not doing so, they are missing an important opportunity to improve each other's life.

Cocking and Kennett, on the other hand, present a different picture of appropriate caring interaction, claiming that there is an important distinction between being a perfectly moral friend and being a perfectly good friend. In order to illustrate this distinction, they offer us the following example:

> Carl, the main character of the film *Death in Brunswick*, is no saint. ... He drinks too much, and he works as a cook at a seedy nightclub in Brunswick... One night, Mustapha, his drug-dealing kitchen hand, is badly beaten up in the back alley by the nightclub heavies. Carl is warned to keep his mouth shut; Mustapha is told that Carl is responsible for the beating. So late that night, Mustapha staggers into the kitchen and lunges at Carl, who is holding a long-pronged fork. Mustapha impales himself on the fork and dies. In a panic, Carl calls his best friend Dave, an easy-going family man. ... Dave dresses and drives to the nightclub to see what is up. His initial response when shown the body is that the police must be called. Carl begs him not to, saying that he could not cope with going to jail. Faced with Carl's fear, Dave takes charge and helps Carl move the body. They take it to the cemetery where Dave works, he breaks into a coffin in an open grave, stamps on the putrefying corpse inside to make room for Mustapha, and re-closes the coffin. Later, they deny all knowledge of Mustapha's disappearance to his distressed widow and son.[17]

Cocking and Kennett claim that although Dave acts immorally in helping his friend Carl, he nonetheless does as he ought to do *as a friend*: he does not act in a morally perfect way, but he acts perfectly as a friend. They claim that Carl, as Dave's close friend, can legitimately expect Dave to help him to act immorally, because that is what good friends ought to do for one another. This is not the moral 'ought' but rather the 'ought' of friendship. Friendship, according to Cocking and Kennett, generates its own reasons, reasons that may conflict with and sometimes outweigh the reasons of morality.

Thus, how friends interpret and interact with each other depends on the characters of the two friends, the situations they find themselves in, and the interplay between their two characters and those situations. Two bad people will probably interact and interpret each other in ways that make each other worse, while two decent people will probably be drawn and interpreted in ways that look much like how Thomas conceives of an appropriately functioning friendship. Friends have reasons to take an interest in what interests and concerns their friends, and what interests and concerns someone depends upon her character. Thus, if my friend is bad, I will have reason to take an interest in certain bad projects. My friend and I may attempt to promote each other's good but, if we have misguided conceptions of what it is to live a good life, we might very well end up harming one another. Concern causes us to do what we judge best for our friends but we might very well be misguided about what is best for them.

2.4 LOVE AND AFFECTION

I have argued that we expect friends to care for each other for their own sakes. But are there other attitudes that friends usually have with respect to one another? Certainly, it is natural for us to say that we love or like or are fond of our friends. In claiming to have such attitudes are we saying something over and above saying that we care about our friends?

The nature of love and how it differs from or is related to attitudes such as liking, fondness, and affection is a highly complex topic. Perhaps love, of these attitudes, comes closest to the kind of concern discussed in section 2.1, although we sometimes talk as though love involves more, perhaps an intense need for the other person or a pressing desire to be with them. Liking, affection, and fondness all connote, as love also seems to do, an enjoyment of the other in some way: pleasure in the other's company, delight in the other's ways of expressing herself, and a capacity to be charmed or engaged by the other. Such attitudes both cause and result from the forms of interaction discussed in section 2.3 and the kinds of self-disclosure discussed in section 2.2. And they all seem to be significant elements of many friendships: our friends are the people we want to be with because we like them.

I am inclined to think that attitudes such as love, affection, etc., need not accompany concern. I do not think that it is uncommon for people to still care about, for example, former lovers or spouses, even if they have ceased to like or have any fondness for them. We often care about family members (siblings, cousins, aunts, uncles) – we are glad to hear of their well-being and successes, saddened by their suffering and failures – but cannot stand to be around them for any significant length of time. We do not take delight in the company of these people in the way that we delight (at least some of the time) in the company of those we regard as friends.

Importantly, just as with concern, liking, fondness, and affection are all independent of various other sorts of positive attitudes that we can have toward people, attitudes such as admiration, respect, and pride. Where Aristotle, given his requirement that complete friends be virtuous people, would claim that friends have all of these attitudes toward one another, I disagree, as clearly Cocking and Kennett would as well given what they say about the example of Dave and Carl.

Of course, it may be psychologically very difficult to retain any kind of affection or liking for a person we regard with contempt or disgust, but it is not impossible. We often say, "I like him in spite of [his lack of scruples, his lack of concern for animals, his thoughtlessness, etc.]," suggesting that love, liking, etc., can persist in accompaniment with various negative attitudes.

As I have said, the analysis of love and related attitudes or emotions is highly complicated, so I cannot pursue that topic any further here.[18] I think, though, that it is important to point out that liking, being fond of, etc., may not be implied by concern and, if they are not, they are an additional important component of the relationship type that we identify as friendship. Indeed, they are often present in frenemy relationships. Two people can be so bound up with one another that they fight, squabble, and bicker. But they remain bound up with one another because, at least at certain times, they take joy in each other's company. There is often some sense of regret at one's frenemy-ish behavior, and this regret can be called forth by thoughts of how the other can make one laugh or by the charm of the other's smile. In other words, in the midst of backstabbing, frenemies remember how much they like each other. Love–hate relationships necessarily involve love and many frenemies are in love–hate relationships with one another.

2.5 FRIENDSHIP AS INTIMACY

Some philosophers of friendship have built their theory of friendship around one of the features that we have discussed in sections 2.1–2.4. For example, Laurence Thomas has regarded mutual self-disclosure as what is definitive of friendship as opposed to other sorts of caring relationships, while Dean Cocking and Jeannette Kennett have given pride of place to mutual shaping and interpretation. Philosophers of friendship have tended to agree that whatever feature is distinctive of friendship, as opposed to other interpersonal relationships, must exist within a context of mutual non-instrumental concern. I think that all of these philosophers of friendship are correct to a certain extent, in so far as they have isolated something important about friendship: they have described important ways in which friends can inter-act in caring ways. Sharing revelations and shaping character are what we think of as acts of intimacy or closeness, but not just any kind of intimacy or closeness: the most shallow, self-righteous, and vindictive of frenemies are often intimate with one another but that closeness is not always indicative of concern. Concerned interactions of some form or another are central to friendship but perhaps they can take any of a myriad of forms, not just the ones described by Thomas and by Cocking and Kennett.

I think that everyone would agree with Aristotle that friend-ship is marked by a kind of mutual concern between the par-ties and that this concern must go beyond what one feels for just any person merely *qua* person. We care more about our friends than we do about just anyone. This concern involves wanting one's friend to do well, although even the best of friends can at times exhibit frenemy-ish attitudes such as jeal-ousy, resentment, or bitterness. This mutual special concern is the setting for the other elements of friendship.

Thomas and Cocking and Kennett offered views about what those other elements are, pointing to self-disclosure and shap-ing and interpretation. But perhaps we should think about those other elements as being able to take any number of forms that can combine in different ways in different friendships. While mutual special concern is necessary for friendship, it is only some combination of some number of the other elements that is required for two people to be friends. So friends will interact in ways that are expressive of their concern for one another, but the forms that that concerned interaction may take do not need to be the sharing of revelations or the shaping and drawing of character. The ways in which two people can show concern for one another can take as many forms as can the people involved in friendship. Further, it may not be clear to anyone outside of the friendship that a particular interaction between the parties is demonstrative of concern because individuals develop, throughout the history of a relationship, unique and private ways of showing that they care. However, the parties to the friendship must recognize that they are expressing concern for one another even if others do not.

And here we can see why we need to be careful not to dismiss all of those who behave in frenemy-ish ways as being something other than genuine friends. People can show their concern for one another in a surprising variety of ways, and bickering and carping is really not an unusual way to do so. Whether it is a healthy way to do so is another matter. Of course, I am inclined to think that in many of the frenemy relationships that we see on reality TV the background of genuine mutual non-instrumental concern is not present, and thus those frenemies are not really friends. But most of those frenemy relationships are between shallow, self-absorbed people: if the parties to a frenemy relationship interact in frenemy-ish ways for different sorts of reasons, they might very well have genuine mutual concern for each other.

Another element common to many friendships is that the parties to the friendship desire to spend time with one

Friendship and Social Media

another. Many of us enjoy the company of our friends and so want to engage in shared activities, such as going to museums, playing golf, or watching movies. In fact, particularly for very close friends, merely spending time together is pleasurable, even if they are not engaging in any particular activity or are not even having a conversation – many people regard it as a mark of being very close to another person that they can enjoy a companionable silence in each other's presence without feeling a need to fill that silence. And spending time together can take place in ways other than face-to-face interaction: friends can use the telephone or Skype in order to interact and spend time together.

Friends also, as a result of their interactions, come to know each other better than they know strangers or mere acquaintances. This knowledge of one another can take many forms and can be gathered in many different ways. Some friends will simply sit and talk over a cup over tea, explicitly telling each other about themselves, their histories, their feelings, their dreams and hopes, etc. Other friends get to know one another through their shared activities, observing each other and piecing together bits of conversation. And the special way in which friends know one another is usually more a matter of having gained understanding through being together rather than an accumulation of data as one might acquire by reading a biography. Friends know what it is like to be with someone when they are vulnerable and open; they know what it is like to laugh at private jokes; they know what it feels like to be comforted or supported by each other. This knowledge often allows friends to be able to engage in that shaping and interpretation of each other to which Cocking and Kennett point: we often say that our friends know us better than we know ourselves because they can locate our self-deceptions and evasions and bring them to light for us. They can read our body language and bring it into contrast with our words, revealing inconsistencies or hidden desires.

Finally, friendship is usually marked by mutual shared attitudes of a positive sort, attitudes usually described as liking, loving, being fond of, or having affection for. These attitudes are, of course, tied to the mutual concern that friends have for one another and perhaps are conceptually linked in some way. What is important is that this family of positive attitudes is distinct from other types of positive attitudes, such as respect and admiration. While it may usually be difficult to sustain fondness or love in the face of, for example, disrespect, it is not impossible. Friends change over the course of a relationship, and they may have started from a position of respect, or at least of a lack of disrespect, but changes in their friend can alter that. However, through interaction and understanding, friends can still sustain concern and love because they see how and why their friend has changed and also are acutely aware of their friend's vulnerability and weaknesses. Thus, friendship can breed an intense compassion that will sustain fondness and concern even through stupidity, thoughtlessness, and even plain wickedness.

Again, we can see why frenemies may actually be friends. We can often be shocked at how two people who bicker and insult each other need to be together and will fiercely come to each other's aid when it is called for. Underlying the surface jealousy and resentment lies love and a desire to be with each other: for whatever reason (again, perhaps not healthy), these persons show their concern in antagonistic ways that may appear unpalatable to others. But, as I have said, people vary so much that we have no reason to suppose that concerned interaction will look the same in all cases.

What I have been trying to capture by pointing to these common features of friendship is the notion of intimacy or of being close to someone. This closeness can occur in relationships that are not friendships, such as that between a captor and her captive: Stockholm syndrome is a form of intimacy in which, through forced interaction, people become dependent upon and knowledgeable about one another. This interaction can thereby create shared understanding and, thereby, compassion. However, this sort of relationship is not friendship because it does not occur against the background of a mutual special concern.[19] Friendship is, then, intimacy expressed through and gained via concerned interaction.[20]

Of course, unlike Aristotle, I have not required that the parties to a friendship be virtuous. Two less-than-fully virtuous people can care about each other and be close to one another, and this is also true of morally bad people as well. Many truly wicked or evil people are probably not capable of friendship because they are not capable of caring about another person non-instrumentally: psychopaths are examples of such persons. However, most bad people are still capable of non-instrumental concern: think, for example, of the ways in which many high-ranking Nazis regarded their families. Although various vices can interfere with the ability to sustain emotional bonds, there is no conceptual impossibility involved in morally bad people being friends.

One element of my view that marks it off from many accounts of friendship is the way in which choice plays a role in the establishment of a friendship. Many people differentiate friends from, for example, family by saying that we choose our friends but we do not choose our family. There is some truth in this, but it is a complicated truth. We do not choose to whom we are related by blood so, in that sense, we do not choose our family. However, we are close to and mutually concerned about only some members of our family, so we are friends with only some members of our family. Some non-blood-related friends are people with whom we initially had no choice about coming into contact. Colleagues and neighbors are such instances. But we always do have a choice over whether we become close to someone. Intimacy requires a certain amount of openness and certain types of interaction, and we are free to hold back from these if we do not want to become close to someone. So while we do not have a choice about who comes into our orbit, we do have a choice about how we interact with them and so about whether we become intimate with them. It is true that we often find ourselves naturally falling into friendship, but doing something without much forethought does not make it a matter about which we did not choose.

However, we can see that any element of genuine choice is lacking in cases of Stockholm syndrome, in the sense that the captive develops attitudes toward her captor that are the result of certain pathological forces of which she is unaware and over which she has no conscious control. Should we insist that intimate relationships are only friendships if the element of choice is present? I am unsure what to say about this, although I am inclined to deny that the element of choice needs to be present. In the case of captor and captive, we might try to convince the rescued captive that her captor is not really her friend, but that is most likely because we do not believe that the captor has non-instrumental concern for her former captive. If we were to rule out all concern and love that have less-than-healthy origins as adequate for friendship, we might very well be ruling out an awful lot of actual concern and love as adequate.

So my friendship as intimacy view understands friendship as intimacy against a background of mutual special concern, where intimacy is characterized by some combination of mutual love, liking, fondness, or affection; mutual special knowledge; mutual desires for time shared; and a history of concerned interaction. Some shaping/interpretation and some sharing of revelations will likely occur in such relationships but they are not, in and of themselves, definitive of friendship; rather, they are forms of concerned interaction or of the acquisition of shared special knowledge. So the friendship as intimacy view will likely understand as friends anyone that Aristotle, Thomas, or Cocking and Kennett would regard as friends, and most likely it will consider as friends some that none of those views would see as such. I think that friendship is an expansive notion and, given the variety of human beings and the ways that they can care about and be close with one another, that we should adopt a fairly loose and open conception of friendship. Alexander Nehamas has pointed out that "the bulk of our interactions with our friends are, at least at first sight, trivial and inconsequential."[21] I think that he is absolutely right, as long as we emphasize the "at least at first sight": the ways in which we express concern for our friends can take so many forms, from sharing jokes to recommending the best lip balm to donating a kidney. We simply cannot pick out any one form of interaction, or even several such forms, as definitive of friendship.

2.6 THE REASONS OF FRIENDSHIP

We saw that Cocking and Kennett understood friendship as generating reasons that compete with other reasons, including moral reasons. But even if we do not build morality into our account of friendship (Aristotle's complete friendship) or into our account of the proper function of friendship (Thomas's view), we need not understand the reasons generated by friendship as somehow different from the reasons that we think of as moral.

Consider again Cocking and Kennett's case of Dave and Carl. They claimed that Dave, in helping Carl to hide the body, did the right thing as a friend but the wrong thing morally speaking. But many people think that friendship makes moral demands on people, that we have what are generally called 'special obligations' to our friends. Special obligations are obligations that we have not to all persons merely in virtue of being persons, but rather to some subset of persons in virtue of the special relationship that we have to those persons. For example, some philosophers think that we have special obligations of promise-keeping: these are obligations to those persons to whom we stand in the special relationship created by the making of a promise to another person or persons. Similarly, then, some philosophers of friendship think that we have special obligations to those persons to whom we stand in the special relationship of friendship.[22]

Consider again the case of Dave and Carl. If we accept that friends have special obligations to care for each other, then we could say that Dave has a special obligation to help Carl to hide the body. In such a case, what Dave would otherwise have no obligation to do becomes obligatory as a result of his relationship with Carl. But of course Dave has other obligations or duties in this case: to report crime to the proper authorities, to ensure that people do not suffer from not knowing what has become of their loved ones, to help everyone – including Carl – to be morally good people, etc. So in order to determine what the all-things-considered morally right action is,

Dave has to weigh all of his obligations against one another and try to figure out which is the strongest in these particular circumstances. In some cases, helping a friend will be the morally right thing to do; in others it will not be the morally right thing to do. Figuring out our all-things-considered obligations in cases as complex as that of Dave and Carl is an extremely difficult task.

We may, then, hold that friendship does not require that its participants be virtuous and also that friendship does not serve a peculiarly moral function, and yet still think that friendship does have moral implications. Such an account can hold that friendship generates special obligations, obligations that compete with our more general duties. The extent to which this claim differs from that put forth by Cocking and Kennett depends upon the extent to which what Cocking and Kennett see as the special reasons of friendship are commensurable with, or weighable against, our moral duties. If they are so commensurable, then there will likely be no difference, practically speaking, between the two views. If they are not, then there will be a practical difference, in so far as, on that view, a person will have to choose between acting as a good friend and acting morally, and there is no way of weighing those choices against one another.

Another important implication of the claim that friends have moral duties to one another, or that they have special reasons of friendship as understood by Cocking and Kennett, is that friends have an obligation or reason to understand what is truly in the other person's interests, i.e. what a good life for her would involve. When we think about the standard cases of frenemies, part of our disapproval of their behavior arises, I believe, from their lack of any genuine understanding of how to live a good life: they tend to be shallow, superficial people.

If one does not know what it is to live a good life, then one's attempts to exhibit concern for a friend will usually backfire because one will not be aiming at what is truly good for one's friend. (Just as one's attempts to care for oneself will backfire because one will be aiming at the wrong sorts of things for oneself.) So our examination of the good life in Chapter Four is not only relevant to assessing how friends can make our lives go better, but also to the determination of what we ought to be doing for our friends.

2.7 FRIENDS, LOVERS, AND OTHER RELATIONS

How is friendship different from or the same as other interpersonal relationships? In particular, how does friendship differ from romantic or sexual relationships and from familial relationships?

In order to answer this question, we need to understand not only what we mean when we talk about friendship but also what we mean when we talk about family relationships and romantic/sexual relationships. Just as with friendship, there are competing accounts of what makes two people members of the same family and of what makes it the case that two people have a romantic or a sexual relationship, so there are no straightforward, uncontested answers to the questions about how all of these types of relationships compare to one another. Nonetheless, we can notice some factors that would need to be brought into any attempt to understand these different relationships.

Family is often understood to involve some sort of biological connection, as is evidenced by the paradigmatic familial relationships: parent/child, siblings, grandparent/grandchild, aunt or uncle/niece or nephew, and cousins. But we also consider some non-biologically related persons to be members of the same family, in particular, spouses and adoptive parents/adopted children. These latter cases are instances of relationships that have a legally defined status. So family seems to involve either biology or some sort of legal recognition of status.

But we also seem to use the term 'family' in cases where we want to stress that someone has become a very important part of our life. In such cases, we will tell that person, "You are not just a friend, you are family." We are clearly not saying that we have discovered a previously unknown biological relationship or that our relationship has become legally recognized. We seem to be indicating some form of deep and lasting commitment, a prioritizing of that person's interests above those of 'mere friends.'

It is unclear, however, that this use of the term 'family' is of any real philosophical interest. When we consider the kinds of connections between persons who are friends that we have been discussing in this chapter, there is no upper limit on the nature and strength of the commitment that the friends can have to one another. In fact, we might think that if familial relationships, either biologically or legally defined, are to have meaning or value for us, then they will have to exhibit at least many of the features pointed to as characteristic of friendship – features such as trust, non-instrumental concern, and intimacy.

Of course, some familial relationships, in particular that between parent and young child, are not characterized by the lack of authority to which some philosophers of friendship point as a requirement of friendship. But equality can develop in such relationships as children grow up and, in the best parent–child relationships, friendship will develop over time, a friendship which could meet the conditions of intimacy. Further, we think that it is unfortunate if such friendship does not develop, indicating that mere family, considered as just biological or legal relation, is not somehow superior to friendship. After all, distant biological relations mean far less to us than do our friends and contribute very little if anything to the value of our lives.

Romantic relationships or sexual relationships seem to involve either an already-existing sexual intimacy or the hope for or striving toward such intimacy. But it seems that in ordinary usage, we do not take the mere addition of sex to friendship to be enough to characterize a relationship as romantic, as is evidenced by our expression 'friends with benefits.' Romance involves some sort of idealization and courting that are not part of friendship as such and, in fact, do not require friendship. Neither, of course, does sexual involvement require friendship. On the other hand, both sex and romance are entirely compatible with friendship and, for most of us, the ideal sexual or romantic relationship, especially long-term sexual or romantic relationship, will involve close friendship. It is when the paradigmatic elements of friendship – trust, intimacy, care – are missing from sexual relationships that such relationships become hurtful, demeaning, or valueless beyond the fleeting sexual pleasure produced. In *The Subjection of Women*, John Stuart Mill claimed that the problem with upper-class marriage in England in the nineteenth-century was that men and women were socialized and educated in such different ways that friendship between marital partners was rare.[23] Without friendship, legal relationships such as marriage can be reduced to nothing more than economic partnerships.

As I said, there is simply not space to completely explore how friendship differs from other sorts of interpersonal relationships, but hopefully this brief discussion shows that, rather than friendship somehow being lesser than family or romantic relationships, the best instances of the latter two types of relationship will involve friendship. Thus, understanding the contributions of friendship to the good life is that much more imperative.

NOTES

1 I borrow the distinction between moralized and non-moralized accounts of friendships from Dean Cocking and Jeanette Kennett, "Friendship and Moral Danger," *Journal of Philosophy* 97:5 (2000), 278–296: 280.

2 *Nichomachean Ethics*: 1156a10ff.

3 The 'only' is important here. Most of us have some instrumental concern for our friends. For example, I care about Richard as a means to my amusement in so far as he can always make me laugh. But such instrumental concern is compatible with non-instrumental concern: I can care about Richard as a means to my amusement and for his own sake.

4 Aristotle would have labeled this sort of relationship a 'friendship for pleasure.' But, of course, pleasure is one kind of advantage we can gain from association with another person, so we can subsume friendships for pleasure under friendships for advantage. Aristotle had reasons for distinguishing the two types of relationship that had to do with what he regarded as lovable for its own sake (see *Nichomachean Ethics*: 1155b20). But these reasons need not concern us here.

5 Although David Velleman makes a valiant, if unconvincing, effort to say that the appropriate object of love is the beloved's Kantian rational agency. See his "Love as a Moral Emotion," *Ethics* 109 (1999), 338–374.

6 How virtuous is a matter of debate, a matter of debate that we need not enter into here. Also, Aristotle did not think that it was literally impossible for virtuous people to degenerate into vicious people, only that their characters were much more stable than those of the non-virtuous.

7 In "Romantic Love and Loving Commitment: Articulating a Modern Ideal," *American Philosophical Quarterly* 33 (1996), 338–374: 344.

8 Delaney puts this as saying that we want various properties to be the grounds but not the object of our love. So Elaine's love for Jerry is rooted in his character or personality, but she loves Jerry, not just the qualities he has. In "Romantic Love and Loving Commitment": 343.

9 *Nichomachean Ethics*: 1156b25.

10 "Friendship," *Synthese* 72 (1987), 217–236: 217.

11 In *Ethics* 108:3 (1998), 502–527.
12 "Friendship and the Self": 505.
13 "Friendship and the Self": 503.
14 Thomas, *Living Morally: A Psychology of Moral Character* (Philadelphia, PA: Temple University Press, 1989): 143.
15 *Living Morally*: 155.
16 *Living Morally*: 156–157.
17 "Friendship and Moral Danger": 279–280.
18 Once again, Helm's entry on "Love" in the *Stanford Encyclopedia of Philosophy* is a good resource for exploring this topic.
19 Although such concern can develop – it is theoretically possible for captor and captive to actually become friends. See the following discussion.
20 For a more complete discussion of intimacy and its consequences for rationality and morality, see my *Rationality and Moral Theory: How Intimacy Generates Reasons* (New York, NY: Routledge, 2008).
21 *On Friendship*: 199.
22 For more on the concept of special obligations, see my entry "Special Obligations" in the *Stanford Encyclopedia of Philosophy* (https://plato.stanford.edu/entries/special-obligations/).
23 John Stuart Mill, *The Subjection of Women* (Indianapolis, IN: Hackett Publishing, 1988).

Three

3.1 MAKING AND KEEPING FRIENDS ON SOCIAL MEDIA

At the beginning of Chapter One, I presented a thought experiment in which, as an expert in non-Earth living, you could undertake your mission to a distant planet either alone, in the company of a stranger, or in the company of a friend. I supposed that most of us would choose the last of those three options: we would choose to spend two years on a distant planet with a friend rather than with a stranger or by ourselves. But, of course, we have to keep in mind that, even if we chose solitude or the company of a stranger, we would be able to contact our friend via e-mail, Skype, Twitter, Instagram, and Facebook (we are just supposing that somehow they have been able to link that distant planet to Earth so that all of these technologies are available for use). To what extent, if any, would the use of such technologies compensate for the lack of the physical presence of a friend?

In this chapter I am going to focus on the advantages and disadvantages of the use of social media (Twitter, Instagram, and, particularly, Facebook) in conducting and sustaining a friendship. Interestingly, in recent years the great majority of philosophical articles that have addressed friendship online have asked whether online technologies allow for the achievement of Aristotelian complete friendship.[1] But many contemporary philosophers of friendship, and, I believe, most non-philosophers, reject this Aristotelian account. So I am going to consider the extent to which use of social media can advance or impede the concern and intimacy that, I have argued in the previous chapter, are what characterize those interpersonal relationships that count as friendships.

It is important to keep in mind that I am not here considering the extent to which use of social media affects the *value* of friendship: that issue will be addressed in Chapter Five, after we have discussed, in Chapter Four, how friendship can and often does contribute to the value of our lives. In the current chapter I am concerned only with the extent to which social media affects the existence and, in particular, the endurance of those elements of a relationship that are relevant to the determination of that relationship as a friendship. It is then a further question as to whether the diminution or enhancement of the intimacy or concern that constitutes a particular friendship causes or constitutes a diminution or enhancement of either the intrinsic or instrumental value of that friendship.

Furthermore, it is undoubtedly true that friendships exist on a continuum in so far as intimacy and concern exist on a continuum. We care more about and are more intimate with some of our friends than we are with others: sometimes this is a matter of the stage of the friendship (perhaps I have been friends with Richard, for example, for over 25 years but with Marcy for only a few months), while at other times it is just a matter of the nature of the friendship (perhaps I have been friends with both Richard and Henry for over 25 years but I have never become as close to Henry as I have become to Richard, nor come to have the same degree of concern for the former that I have for the latter). And friendships can develop in both directions, i.e. sometimes we get closer to a friend and sometimes a previous intimacy has attenuated over time. So, apart from issues about how social media affects the value of a friendship, there are important issues about how social media impacts the degree of intimacy and concern that we have for a friend. It is this latter issue with which I am primarily concerned in this chapter because, as we avail ourselves of social media in our friendships, I believe we need to be attentive to how such usage might change the very nature of those friendships.

In considering this issue, I am going to focus on the role that embodiment plays in intimacy and in concern. As I said in first discussing the mission to a distant planet, even when we are in touch with friends on social media, it is not uncommon for us to long for their physical company, to see them in person – to get together with them and to just 'hang out.' Whatever the ills of being alone, it seems – at least for many of us – that they are not entirely cured via the virtual presence of a friend. Is this fact just the result of an unfortunate pre-technological habituation to physical company, such that we ought to attempt to overcome it? Or is it the case that if we were to cease to long for and to seek out the physical presence of friends, we would thereby be reducing the very intimacy and concern that are constitutive of friendship?

My focus is going to be on relationships in which the parties to the friendship have already interacted with one another face-to-face, whether that face-to-face interaction is what initiated the friendship or occurred after an online meeting. There is, of course, a distinct issue concerning whether genuine friendships can be formed and maintained without any face-to-face interaction and, in considering the challenges of using social media in conducting relationships with at least some face-to-face component, hopefully we can shed some light on the challenges and opportunities of entirely virtual relationships. But my concern will be on relationships with at least some face-to-face component, because it seems that those remain the most common kind of relationship in which social media plays a part. These are also the kinds of relationships for which the virtues of social media have been most heralded: it is said that we can keep in better touch with geographically distant friends, reconnect with friends with whom we have lost contact, and find a larger circle of (eventually face-to-face) friends with common interests.

Social media is supposed to allow us to create and maintain friendships that we could not or would find difficult to create or maintain without it. And here, I think, Sharon Vallor puts the central issue well, by comparing the maintenance of friendship with maintaining a garden:

> I might speak of "maintaining" my garden, when by this I mean throwing enough water on it just often enough to keep it limping along, or I might refer to my sustained and careful efforts to nourish and tend to it lovingly, to ensure that every part of it not only lives, but thrives.[2]

To what extent can social media enhance and strengthen friendship, and to what extent can it impede or weaken friendship?

My own account of friendship understood in terms of intimacy views friendship as a complex relationship the features of which, while having certain commonalities from one such relationship to another, nonetheless are dependent for their nature upon the particularities of the parties and their circumstances. Thus, not surprisingly, the ways in which social media impacts friendship will also differ from one friendship to another. So my conclusions in this chapter do not constitute any sort of definitive judgments about the role of social media in friendship. Rather, I aim to outline both possible pitfalls and advantages of such use within the context of friendship, and then each of us can examine what, if any, would be the best way of incorporating or avoiding social media in our own friendships, where even for a single person the best way may differ from one friendship to another. By seeing possible pros and cons of social media employment in friendship, I hope to suggest that we at least need to be more thoughtful in choosing our modes of interaction: we now have more and more varied ways of responding to friends but that does not mean that we should employ them all in all of our relationships.

In examining uses and misuses of social media in friendship, I will focus on the same features that I discussed in the previous chapter: special knowledge, appropriate interaction and responsiveness, and love and concern. As I have already said, I will focus on the role of embodiment in friendship. Physical presence is usually taken as necessary for romantic or sexual relationships,[3] for obvious reasons, but often friendship is sharply contrasted with such relationships in so far as it is seen as lacking an erotic component. I argue, however, that the lack of sex or sexual attraction in a relationship does not equate to a lack of physical attraction and need of a different sort. I will conclude the chapter by considering the role of such physicality in creating the unique or special bond that exists between friends: while friendships are not exclusive in the sense that one need not (and, in most cases, ought not) limit oneself to one friend, their role in our lives often depends on their having certain unique features that make each one special and non-interchangeable with the others that one has. We need, then, to consider whether social media use can undermine that quality of friendships. (Then, later, in Chapter Five, we can consider whether undermining that quality constitutes or leads to a diminution in value.)

3.2 READING OUR FRIENDS

We know our friends better than we know people who are strangers or mere acquaintances, and, it seems, each of us knows a particular friend in a way that no one else knows her. This special knowledge that friends have of each other is at least part of the basis for the concern, love, and affection that exists between them: it is part of what we include in the notion of being close to a friend. As I argued in Chapter Two, this knowledge is not just a cataloging of facts or secrets, such as a paparazzi might acquire by constantly following and reading every article about and biography of a celebrity. Rather, it is a knowledge acquired from particular forms of interaction and importantly involves an experiential component: we know what it is like to be comforted by a friend, to laugh at a private joke with a friend, to sit quietly in the company of a friend, to be with third parties together, etc. I think that it is better to say of our friends that perhaps we do not know them 'better' than anyone else does, but we know them in a way that no one else does.

Many of us have had the experience of coming to learn about ourselves by our friends' interpretations of us. For example, suppose that Amanda sincerely believes and asserts that she is not attracted to Frank. But her friend Maddy is familiar with the way that Amanda behaves in various social circumstances, and she notices that Amanda is more-than-usually anxious when in Frank's company, laughs at all of Frank's jokes, even those jokes which Maddy knows that Amanda is not likely to find funny if told by someone other than Frank, and puts more-than-usual effort into choosing her clothing when she knows that she will be seeing Frank. Amanda might then come to realize that she really is attracted to Frank when Maddy points to these facets of Amanda's behavior, pointing out that she, Maddy, noticed similar behavioral shifts the last time that Amanda was attracted to someone. Friends learn how to read our behavior, both as a result of familiarity and as a result of concern: in caring about us, they are inclined to pay more attention to subtle ways that we have of expressing ourselves in order to try to discern our needs. Also, affection is often the result of what others might see as trivial: the way that one frowns when confronted with a particular piece of idiocy, the look that one gets when bored by a conversation but is trying not to reveal it, the different ways in which one laughs in different sorts of amusing situations, etc. As Cocking and Kennett rightly emphasize, who we are and who we understand ourselves as being are at least in part a result of interacting with our friends and having our friends then relay back to us their own takes on those interactions and on other behaviors we exhibit.

This aspect of face-to-face interaction with friends has been one of the main bones of contention with respect to the possibilities of online friendship. As Cocking and Matthews point out, social media depends upon voluntary as opposed to non-voluntary self-disclosure, and so it seems that we have a great deal of choice and control in how we present ourselves online.[4] Consider a stereotypical example: Anna is a 20-year-old college student. If we were to look at Anna's Facebook page, we would see pictures of Anna serving food at a soup kitchen, attending rallies in support of racial equality, and spending time with her family. Her comments are all about how black lives matter, the need to end poverty, and the importance of family. Anna has portrayed herself as a loving member of her family deeply committed to social justice. But Anna, as with many people on Facebook, has been very, very selective about what she has posted. She has not posted a picture of the latest screaming match with her mother that resulted from her mother's unwillingness to buy her an expensive designer purse. And she has not posted any pictures from the bar crawl where she ended the night vomiting into the gutter. Anna has carefully crafted an online persona so as to project an image of herself that she wants others to see (and, perhaps, that she herself wants to see). Returning to our previous example, social media, then, would allow Amanda to maintain the fiction that she is not attracted to Frank, a fiction that, in our hypothetical, she could not maintain in face-to-face interaction with her friend Maddy.

But as I said, the example of Anna the college student is stereotypical, although I have no doubt that many people craft their online images in the way that I have imagined Anna as doing. Even if, however, one is simply trying to relay information to friends and not consciously trying to create a persona, there is a process of selection that must go into deciding what to say in one's posts and which pictures to put on one's page. But, of course, a process of selection goes into what we say and do in face-to-face interaction as well. And perhaps there are advantages to the kind of selection process that is prompted by social media. Adam Briggle argues that the shields provided by being online offer advantages not available in face-to-face interaction: we can be more deliberate and thoughtful as we take time to express ourselves, and we can be more open given that we have the buffer of the virtual world.[5] So as long as there is some face-to-face interaction in a friendship, that buffer can simply allow us to offer more to our friends so that they have more pieces to the puzzle. So the debate between Cocking and Matthews and Briggle may be at a draw: we acquire some kinds of knowledge more readily in face-to-face interaction, and other kinds more readily when there is a digital buffer in place. (I will return to this issue about a buffer in Chapter Five.)

The problem with the debate, however, is that it focuses on information about a friend and how that information can or cannot be acquired. So Cocking and Matthews point out that we often learn facts about our friends from observation, and these are facts about themselves that our friends only reveal involuntarily. Briggle, on the other hand, emphasizes that not being face-to-face may make us more willing to offer certain kinds of voluntary revelations. But all of this ignores an important aspect of the knowledge that we have with respect to our friends, namely that that knowledge goes beyond the kind of information that could be put into a comprehensive biography. Consider a case in which something funny has happened to you, and then think about the difference between conveying that incident to a friend via social media and conveying that incident to that same friend in person. You know what it would be like to be able to laugh together with your friend in person, and you know that that experience would be very different than posting a description of that incident and then getting 'LOL' as a reply. Does intimacy require the former kind of knowledge? Whether or not it is strictly required, it certainly enhances it. We know ourselves as embodied beings, and it certainly seems that closeness to a friend can only be enhanced if they also know us as such.

Another important difficulty with social media use is not its prevention of our ability to read our friends or to have certain kinds of experiential knowledge (at least not for re-lationships with at least some face-to-face component), but rather the ways in which it can blur boundaries both between the intimate sphere and the public sphere and also between different intimate spheres within our lives. Much is often made of the fact that friendship, unlike traditional Western romantic or sexual relationships, is not exclusive, and that, in fact, we think that it is best if people have more than one close friend. But friendship, at least close friendship, none-theless has its own type of exclusivity: what differentiates one friendship from another is the way in which the parties have interacted, and this includes what they have divulged to one another and how those revelations have both been received by the other and been reflected back after having been in-corporated into the other's interpretation of her friend and shaping of herself. There is a danger in sharing too much with too many people: the information is not aimed at any one particular person, has not been crafted or shaped for her par-ticular consumption, and often responses to that information, given the amount that we need to process and the nature of social media, become conventional – we 'like' posts, send a 'thumbs-up' emoji, say "Hang in there" – and that conven-tional response is one among many of the same sort that is received.

Friendships require time and energy if we are to craft a unique bond based on both unconscious and conscious rev-elations, revelations that then shape how we move forward together. But then we need to have boundaries that define each of the relationships in our lives. Many people recognize this fact, and so utilize features of, for example, Facebook, that allow them to have private postings and exchanges, and also make sure to communicate with close friends through supplementary venues such as e-mail and Skype. The special way of knowing that exists between two friends is not just a function of what each reveals to the other, but of how those revelations interact with one another, how they shape future revelations, how they shape and are shaped by the other kinds of caring interactions that occur, etc. Mass communications, especially if they utilize conventional forms such as 'likes' or emojis, simply do not have the same causal powers as individualized ones. So over- or misuse of social media can reduce the intimacy that is characteristic of friendship by reducing the special knowledge that friends have of one another, even as it might increase the sheer quantity of information that they have.[6]

3.3 RESPONDING AND CARING

Another important feature of the intimacy characteristic of friendship is the distinctive way in which we respond to and interact with a friend, a way of responding and interacting that is attentive to a friend's needs and concerns and that aims at the promotion of the friend's well-being.[7] This attentiveness and promotion of well-being require empathy if they are to be effective, i.e. if we are to actually understand our friends' needs and concerns and to discern the appropriate way to respond to them. Empathy is a matter of putting ourselves in the other's shoes, of seeing the matter as she does, and of feeling as she does. How well can we do this via interaction on social media?

There has been a lot of empirical research on the physical mechanisms that underlie our empathetic capacities.[8] An important upshot of this research is the importance of physical cues to activating our empathy. The most primitive forms of empathy involve mirroring, where the body language (gestures, posture, facial expressions, etc.) are picked up via 'contagion': they are transmitted through an unconscious process in the way that yawns or laughter can be.[9] More active forms of empathy involve either consciously reflecting on our unconscious mirroring of the other or consciously projecting ourselves into the situation and mind-set of the other. The fuller the picture we have of the other, in the sense of knowing about her situation and her conscious and unconscious reactions to it, the better we can empathize with her, either in the primitive sense or in one of the more reflective, conscious ways.

And of course the fuller the picture that we have of the other, the more appropriately we can respond to her in a way that is not only expressive of concern but is effective, in the sense of having the other understand our expression of concern as being what it is, this latter being very important in maintaining the love and care that the parties have for another. In immediate face-to-face interaction, we can get a multitude of behavioral cues about how the other is responding to what we are saying or doing that we cannot get via postings on social media. How the other reacts in an immediate and non-reflective way is often relevant to understanding her, in a way that her carefully thought-out responses on social media may not be. We often need to know how our friend actually feels about what we have said or done, not just how she thinks it is appropriate for her to feel, and we cannot get that knowledge if there is a buffer between us.[10]

We can, then, see the importance of face-to-face interaction to having the very strong empathy that is both requisite to and part of the intimacy between friends. Part of what it is to be emotionally close to someone is to pick up more quickly and effectively on how she is feeling than we do with those with whom we are not close. This empathy is both guided by and guides our concern and our expressions of concern for the other. Its development once again points up the importance to friendship of what can appear trivial: to build a picture of another person, we need to see her in ordinary moments just as much as we need to see her in extraordinary moments. To interpret behavior as unusual or out of character, we need to know what is in character, and so we need to know how someone acts and reacts in ordinary, everyday circumstances.

I think that the conclusion for social media employment in friendship is obvious: the richness of intimate and emotionally engaged interaction with and responsiveness to friends is, at least in part, a function of being in the bodily presence of friends. Of course, then, if social media is only one element of a friendship, we might think that it poses no difficulties for the sustaining of the deep empathetic interaction between friends, because it exists only as a supplement to more traditional modes of interaction. But I am not so sure that this is the case.

If we use social media and other forms of digital interaction to supplement a face-to-face friendship, we face the issue of integrating the two forms of interaction. As we have seen, there are different kinds of barriers in the different forms of interaction: on social media we miss various cues from body language, while in face-to-face interaction, we may feel less comfortable making certain types of admission to each other (at least at the beginning of a friendship). But let us imagine a case of two friends, Linus and Sally, who have known each other for several years. At first their interactions were always face-to-face, but recently, as a result of busy family and work lives, they have been in touch only on social media. They have read each other's posts, posted on each other's pages, and viewed photos and videos. When they finally manage to get together, will their interaction be enhanced or impeded by the intervening social media contact?

As with all matters in this realm, there are no necessary truths about the effect on a relationship of a period of online-only engagement. As I said in the first section of this chapter, my aim is only to point to possible advantages and disadvantages. One obvious potential advantage is that Linus and Sally have a background of information about each other that they can take as given, and can spend their time together moving forward, as it were, or focusing only on what really matters. As an analogy, consider taking a course on twentieth-century American literature. The course will proceed very differently if everyone involved knows that everyone else has already taken the course on nineteenth-century American literature: the professor need not rehash the plot of, say, *The Adventures of Huckleberry Finn*, or explain various interpretations of the relationship between Ahab and the whale in *Moby Dick*. Thus, the course has a background of shared knowledge that they can draw on to enhance but not slow down their study of Fitzgerald and Faulkner.

But I think that the current twentieth-century course would be very different if all of the students had not only taken the nineteenth-century course but had taken it together. In engaging with the novels together, they would have heard and responded to each other's reactions to the novels and to each other's responses to their reactions. Those reactions would have been (in an ideal classroom situation, at least) modified and shaped by their discussions with one another. So, inevitably, their interactions in the current course would be imbued with the give-and-take of the previous course, and thus would have a very different character than if, say, they had simply read each other's online posts about how they felt and what they thought about the various nineteenth-century novels.

I imagine that this discussion of the students in the literature classes reminded you of the previous chapter's discussion of the shaping and interpretation characteristic of many friendships. And I think that the import for Sally and Linus is clear. If they had been meeting in regular face-to-face interactions rather than only via social media, not only would they have shared information about each other, but how they went forward with that information would have been, most likely, richer and deeper. Linus would have asked Sally for more information about her dismissive attitude toward her new co-worker, sensing from her body language that there is more to the story than just a judgment of incompetence. Sally would have noticed Linus blush when he was asked how his recent academic conference presentation went, and she might have challenged him about his recent political leanings in a way that she avoided doing on Facebook because she did not want to come across as hostile. And when Sally speaks about her grandmother's death, Linus can put an arm around her and pull her close to him, being there for her in a way that online interaction obviously does not allow. Sally can then admit that she actually feels conflicted about that death, because it had been a long time coming and the trips to the care center had become burdensome: this is not the kind of admission she would be likely to make online for fear of misunderstanding and of negative responses. But with Linus she can indicate that she feels awful about being conflicted and convey via her expression how much she loved her grandmother. I do not think that we can really doubt that social media interaction as opposed to face-to-face interaction gives a different sort of character to a friendship, and, I would suggest, in general, it will give it a less deep and less rich character.

In fact, I am not sure that we can really count a lot of social media usage as actual interaction between friends. The most commonly used features of Facebook are those that are not created with a single person in mind: we post to our pages, intending for all of our friends to read what we write or to view our photos or videos. The mere fact that Lucy peruses Charlie's posts does not count as the kind of caring interaction characteristic of friendship; in fact, it more closely approximates the reading of a biography or an article about a celebrity in *People* magazine. As an analogy, consider the difference between a friend buying a gift specifically for you, and that same friend putting various items on a table at a party and inviting the various guests to choose something before they leave. The former gift is a much more meaningful expression of concern because of the thought about you specifically that went into its choice and purchase. The table full of gifts is still thoughtful but it is not expressive of the same kind of particularistic concern. Most Facebook, Twitter, etc., posts are like the table full of gifts: nice to receive, but not expressive of the same kind of particularistic concern as is interaction directed specifically to and with a particular individual in mind.

Of course, nothing that I have said here is an argument against reflective use of social media, especially when we are distant from friends. But given how much time many of us spend on social media, we need to make a concerted effort not to forgo face-to-face or other forms of one-on-one interaction with friends if we are to sustain a history of concerned interaction.

3.4 LOVE AND AFFECTION IN DIGITAL SPACE

As I have already pointed out, we take for granted the importance of the body in romantic and sexual relationships because we take it for granted that those relationships have an erotic component. But there has been a tendency in both philosophical and non-philosophical discourse to downplay the role of the physical body in 'mere' friendship. We tout the best friendships as a 'meeting of the minds (or spirits),' as relationships where physical appearance is irrelevant. Supposedly, in the best friendships, we can get to what is truly essential about the other person, where what is essential is understood to be her character, her personality, and her inner life more generally.

Thus, it might be thought, and has been said by some philosophers talking about the possibility of attaining Aristotelian complete friendship online, that social media and other forms of digital interaction allow us to bypass physical barriers to intimacy. So off-putting or socially stigmatized physical characteristics, or features such as race that can call forth hidden biases, will not serve as blocks to connection and understanding between two people. And so it might be that we can initiate certain friendships online that we would never be able to initiate in person.

But I think that affection and love, even in friendships without an erotic component, can rarely be divorced from the physical embodiment of the object of the love or affection, at least for the great majority of us. When I think about my friends, my feelings of affection for them get called forth by thoughts of the way that they smile when they see me, the way in which they express boredom or frustration, the way that they laugh at stupid jokes, the ways in which they can evoke cherished memories with a look or a gesture, etc. It is remarkable how much of our understanding and sense of another person comes from apparently trivial features such as how blissed-out how he looks when he eats cherry pie, how she cuddles her cat, how she frowns in absorption when reading an engrossing book, etc.

Why do these physical quirks and expressions deepen our love and affection? This is an extraordinarily difficult question but at least one explanation, I am inclined to believe, is that the other person's physical embodiment is a tangible and effective reminder of her vulnerability and need. The bottom line is that we are not disembodied minds, free from the constraints of this earthly realm, and we wear our lives on our faces and on our bodies. There is just a difference between the kind of affection or love that can develop online unimpeded by bodily intervention, and the kind of affection or love that develops in response to an entire person. It is true that we live in a society which is superficial and obsessed with physical beauty, and so I agree with some commentators that there is an attraction to being able to connect with someone without having to worry about whether they are judging our physical appearance or having their judgments of our character, intellect, and personality mediated by their judgments of our physical beauty or lack thereof. On the other hand, my most deeply loving and affectionate relationships are those in which I know that my friend loves me entirely, loving even those physical characteristics that are not conventionally attractive but are expressive of my attitudes and character.

I think that a good example of how physicality plays into affection is provided by the film *The Third Man*. In the film, we meet Holly Martins, whose good friend Harry Lime is supposedly dead. During the first portion of the film, we learn about Harry only through what others, in particular Holly and Harry's lover Anna, say about Harry. When we, along with Holly, finally spy Harry grinning in a doorway, our picture of Harry and of both Holly and Anna's love for him is deepened, because we know that that love was, in part, a response to something about Harry that could only be conveyed by his physical charm. If we now re-watch the earlier discussions about Harry with that physical image in mind, we have a different and richer picture of the affection that each of the other characters has for Harry.

In a similar vein, consider your different reactions to getting, in response to a joke that you post on your Facebook page, 'LOL' from a stranger, from a new friend, and from a very close friend. Your reactions, I am sure, will be quite different. In particular, in the latter case of the close friend, the 'LOL' will evoke, in your mind, different occasions when you have seen your friend wince at how lame your joke is, or suddenly laugh helplessly with a gesture indicating that she is not even really sure why she is laughing. The different 'LOL' responses evoke different reactions in you, with the fullest and deepest reaction being the one that involves relishing the way in which your friend is probably physically reacting to your post.

But overuse of social media, particularly in the sense of having too many 'friends' posting responses to your own posts, will almost inevitably alter the nature of how each response affects you. In order to call up all of the affectionate associations that your close friend's response evokes, you need to dedicate time and imagination to reflecting on that post and on what was likely happening with your friend while she posted. Social media, however, is not conducive to this kind of time deployment: in fact, most of us use it because it requires less effort than face-to-face interaction requires. But if physicality plays the role that I am suggesting in sustaining and strengthening affection, then social media use is not conducive to sustaining and strengthening affection.

But what about the posting of photos and videos? Don't they fill in the gap that textual responses leave open? To some extent, I think that photos and videos can help in sustaining affection but, of course, they have limitations. I know for a fact that how I come across in photographs and videos is quite different than how I am naturally in one-on-one conversation with a friend. In that one-on-one conversation, I am focused on my friend, crafting – in more or less conscious ways – what I say and how I move or sit in response to what she is saying or doing. With photographs and videos there is a barrier, a barrier created by my own self-consciousness and the lack of an immediate interlocutor. This, of course, will vary from one person to another. However, this variance in response merely highlights my overall theme: we need to monitor carefully how social media usage works for us as individuals in each of our particular friendships.

Finally, I think that we need to take note of the way in which one of the most lamented impacts of Facebook might affect the affection and love needed for friendship. Study after study has revealed that an individual's Facebook use correlates with a decline in her well-being: the more one uses Facebook, the less happy one appears to be.[11] While there are varied explanations for this apparent fact, the most often cited is that Facebook leads us to constantly compare our own lives to those of others. We carefully curate our Facebook pages and Twitter feeds, focusing on what we know will appear interesting and enviable to others: a vacation to the Greek isles, a new car, a book contract, front-row seats at a Broadway musical, etc. We do not post about mundane or less-than-enviable aspects of our lives: the article that has been rejected five times, the struggle to find a pair of jeans that fits and looks good, the urinary tract infection that led to the emergency room, and the bitter quarrels with our family. Thus, the online world leads us to see the lives of others as being better than our own: we see only the best aspects of theirs but are fully aware of all the aspects of ours, both the good and the bad.

So Facebook causes us to feel envious, inadequate, and competitive. But of whom are we envious and competitive? Against whom do we feel that we do not measure up? Our friends, of course. But these sorts of reactions to our friends and to their lives are not exactly conducive to sustaining love and affection. There is the danger that I come to see my friends as instruments to point up my own inadequacies and the banality and boredom of my life. In order to avoid feeling this way, I try to look as good as my friends, and the vicious cycle continues. Again, this is only one potential way to use Facebook, but it appears to be a not uncommon way, and clearly poses a danger to both intimacy and affection.

3.5 MAINTAINING A UNIQUE BOND

We live in an age of mass production and of mass consumption. One of the greatest dangers of social media usage for friendship is that it renders friendship itself something to be mass produced and mass consumed. The most used features of social media such as Facebook are those features which allow us to post text and images that are available to the whole gamut of those whom we have 'friended,' where that number averages somewhere over 100 persons. So what we share with those who are supposedly our closest friends is also shared with those with whom we are not so close, with those with whom we are merely acquainted, and even with some who we have never met. Most often, how our 'friends' respond to our posts is also available for consumption by all of our other 'friends.' On social media, our arena of interaction with our friends is open and available to a multitude of persons.

Does this availability to all affect the intimacy between two people? Jeffrey H. Reiman has argued that answering 'yes' to this question "suggests a market conception of personal intimacy":

> The value and substance of intimacy … lies not merely in what I have but essentially in what others do *not* have. The reality of my intimacy with you is constituted not simply by the quality and intensity of what we share, but by its unavailability to others – in other words, by its scarcity.[12]

Reiman was writing before the advent of social media, but his remarks could be used to support the claim that the openness of social media does not equate to a diminution of intimacy. Just because I share more with more people, my bond with my close friend remains precisely what it is.

However, I think that Reiman's remarks are not sufficiently attuned to the way in which intimacy is determined not just by what is revealed on either side, but on how those revelations shape the friends and thus shape their future interactions with each other. If future revelations on Facebook are directed at a multitude, then those revelations have not been appropriately causally affected by interaction with any particular other so as to constitute part of an intimate bond with that other. Intimacy is crafted by interactions that lead to special knowledge, which in turn leads to distinctive forms of further interaction expressive of concern and love. If too many 'interactions' with another are not directed specifically at that person and are shared with many others, then it is very difficult, I think, for the two people involved to create or sustain intimacy.

One of the great dangers of social media, I believe, is that it can give a false sense of intimacy, by providing us with an abundance of information about our friends. But information must be embedded in interaction in significant ways for it to be relevant to the existence of an intimate bond between two people. Intimacy requires unique interconnection: it is not just a matter of being 'kept in the loop.' So while social media can be used to supplement face-to-face interaction in useful ways, it also poses grave dangers to the maintenance of intimacy, and so we need to monitor its usage carefully if we are to maintain friendships in the digital age.

NOTES

1 See the volume of Ethics and Information Technology 14 (2012) which is dedicated to, as the editors of the volume put it, "the question of whether there are obstacles presented by online communication environments for achieving ideal companion friendship" (in the contribution to the volume by Dean Cocking, Jeroen van den Hoven, and Job Timmermans, "Introduction: One Thousand Friends," 179–184: 179). Four out of the five contributions focus on Aristotle's conception of complete friendship as what is understood by "ideal companion friendship."

2 Sharon Vallor, "Flourishing on Facebook: Virtue Friendship and New Social Media," Ethics and Information Technology 14 (2012), 185–199: 198.

3 I say 'usually' because new forms of sexual interaction have arisen with the creation of new digital technologies. How increasing use of these new modes of sexual interaction affects our understanding of romantic and/or sexual interaction is an interesting topic, but not one that we can address here.

4 In "Unreal Friends": 227–228.

5 In "Real Friends: How the Internet can Foster Friendship," Ethics and Information Technology 10 (2008), 71–79: 75, 77. See also Johnny Hartz

Soraker, "How Shall I Compare Thee? Comparing the Prudential Value of Actual and Virtual Friendship," *Ethics and Information Technology* 14 (2012), 209–219: 215.

6 For an interesting discussion of exclusivity and intimacy, and how these features are related to the importance of privacy, see Jeffrey H. Reiman, "Privacy, Intimacy, and Personhood," *Philosophy and Public Affairs* 6 (1976), 26–44.

7 This kind of caring attentiveness need not take the form of dramatic gestures. For example, merely listening carefully to a friend in conversation is a way of showing care, as is recalling and recounting a joke that we committed to memory because we knew that it would amuse her.

8 For a good overview of this research see the introduction to Amy Coplan and Peter Goldie (eds), *Empathy: Philosophical and Psychological Perspectives* (Oxford: Oxford University Press, 2014). In addition to Coplan and Goldie's useful introduction, the articles in the first part of this anthology provide further reading on recent empirical work on empathy.

9 Observation of this phenomena goes back at least to David Hume and Adam Smith's discussions of our sympathy with our fellow human beings.

10 For this reason, I am more inclined to side with Cocking and Matthews than with Briggle in the debate that I mentioned in the previous section.

11 For a brief summary of one of the most recent such studies, see Holly B. Shakya and Nicholas A. Christakis, "A New, More Rigorous Study Confirms: The More You Use Facebook, the Worse You Feel," *Harvard Business Review* online, April 10, 2017.

12 "Privacy, Intimacy, and Personhood": 32.

Four

Suppose that you and a companion, Robinson, are hiking in the desert and you come upon a hut inhabited by a hermit named Herman. Herman has lived alone for many years, meditating and contemplating reality. He tells you that he has no friends and in fact does not want any: he left friendship behind when he moved to his hut in the desert. When you ask Herman whether he regrets this decision, he replies that he does not because he is quite happy and thinks that his life is valuable and well worth living. Robinson, impressed with Herman, tells you that he is thinking of emulating him by finding an equally remote spot to build his own hut and live in solitude without friends. When he asks what you think of his plan, what do you say?

I think most of us would respond to Robinson's plan in the same way: we would tell him that it is a truly lousy plan! When Robinson asks us to explain our judgment, we will point out to him all of the ways that friends enhance our lives. Most obviously, friends provide us with a great deal of pleasure because we enjoy spending time in their company and engaging in various activities, such as going hiking in the desert, with them. They alleviate our pain by providing solace and comfort in difficult times, and they aid us in carrying out both trivial and non-trivial elements of our life plans by, for example, watering our plants when we are out of town and reading drafts of our books or articles. They encourage us to use our talents and they help us to understand ourselves.

Suppose, though, that Robinson points out that what we have shown him is that friendship, at least a good deal of the time, brings us other goods such as pleasure and self-knowledge. But, Robinson points out, Herman has achieved those goods through meditation and reflection. Does Herman, then, and potentially Robinson, have no need for friendship? Is friendship worth having for its own sake or only because there are other things worth having for their own sake, such that most of us, unlike Herman, can only get those other things by having friends? Friendship is clearly, with respect to most of our lives, instrumentally valuable, but is it intrinsically valuable?

In this chapter I will consider how friendship can (and, of course, often does) contribute to living a good life by considering both its instrumental value, i.e. by considering the good things that friendship produces, but also by arguing that friendship is plausibly understood as having intrinsic value. It is important to always keep in mind that the claim that friendship has intrinsic value does not imply either of the necessity claims that we discussed in Chapter One:

> **Necessity of friends:** Necessarily, if a person lacks friends, then that person is not leading a good life.

> **Better with friends:** Necessarily, if a person has at least one friend, then that person has a better life than she would if she lacked friends (holding everything else about her life constant).

If friendship has intrinsic value, then in adding a friend to a life, necessarily, value is added. But something that has intrinsic value may also be instrumentally bad, i.e. it may have intrinsically bad consequences. For example, the pleasure that someone gets from smoking can cause her to continue smoking, which then leads to health issues such as emphysema. However, if friendship has intrinsic value, and it is usually accompanied by good consequences (that may be very difficult to get in any other way) that outweigh its bad consequences, we will be able to conclude that it is generally rational, in the prudential sense (i.e. considering only our own good) to pursue at least some friendships.

In this chapter, after considering in sections 4.1–4.4 the instrumental and intrinsic value of friendship, I will consider the connection between friendship and morality (4.5) and also the connection between friendship and rationality (4.6), considered in the broadest sense as acting on the balance of one's practical reasons. Even if one can live a good life without friends, I argue, there are other ways that friends contribute to our lives, because what it is rational or moral for us to do goes beyond the pursuit of a valuable life for ourselves. What is important or significant cannot be equated with what is good for us or what makes our lives more valuable. While it is important to consider how friendship makes our lives go better, it is also important to keep in mind other ways in which friendship is relevant to our deliberations about how to feel, to think, and to act.

4.1 VALUE AND ITS INCARNATIONS

4.1.1 Intrinsic vs instrumental value

Before considering the ways in which friendship contributes to a valuable life, we need to equip ourselves with some important distinctions that philosophers have employed in theorizing about the nature of value. In Chapter One I introduced the distinction between intrinsic and instrumental value:

> **Intrinsic value and instrumental value:** To say that X has intrinsic value is to say that X is valuable for its own sake, or as an end. To say that X has instrumental value is to say that X is a means to the production of something that has intrinsic value.

In considering the ways in which friendship might make our lives more valuable, we need to consider both its instrumental and its intrinsic value. Friendship, it seems obvious, often has good consequences, and in section 4.2 we will examine three of the potentially many such that friendship can, and often does, produce: pleasure, self-knowledge, and self-development. For each of these goods that friendship produces, there will arise the question: is it intrinsically or instrumentally valuable? In order for friendship to be instrumentally valuable, it does not matter what the answer to that question is: as long as friendship leads ultimately, either directly or indirectly, to something of intrinsic value, then it is instrumentally valuable.

Does friendship itself have intrinsic value? Does it have value regardless of whether it produces pleasure, self-knowledge, self-development, or anything else of either intrinsic or instrumental value? It is, I think, always difficult to defend any claim to the effect that something has intrinsic value. First, we need to be able to isolate the thing that we are considering, in this case friendship, from all of its standard consequences, and this is often quite challenging: when I think about my friendships, I almost inevitably think about how much I enjoy the company of my friends, how they have supported me in my career, how they have offered comfort in hard times, etc. How can I think about a friendship apart from all of the effects, distinct from itself, that it has on my life? We can try to employ the so-called 'isolation test' in order to determine whether something, X, has intrinsic value: consider a world in which X does not exist, and then compare that with a world that is exactly the same as the first world except in so far as X is now added to the world. As we noted in Chapter One, however, it is extraordinarily difficult to add a friendship to a world and still leave everything else constant, but I think we have to try to accomplish this task in order to decide for ourselves whether friendship has intrinsic value.

Second, even if I manage this task, what sort of argument can I give to someone else in order to convince her that friendship is (or is not) intrinsically valuable? We can encourage her to perform the isolation test, but what if she claims that the addition of X makes the world no more valuable while, after engaging in the test, we claim that it does? I am not sure that there is anything else that we can do at this point, except to reconsider the two worlds and to encourage our disputant to do the same. After all, something's having intrinsic value is a matter of the nature of the thing, considered in and of itself, and so pointing to something beyond that thing is irrelevant.

However, one way in which philosophers have attempted to argue for the claim that a certain activity, object, or relationship is an intrinsic part of a good life for a human person is to examine the nature of the human person and attempt to somehow link up the proposed activity, etc., to what seems plausibly an excellent or worthwhile life for a being of that nature. This approach is famously used by Aristotle and, at least to an extent, by John Stuart Mill. Of course, in order to convince ourselves or another that friendship is intrinsically good using this approach, we need to have some prior understanding not only of the 'nature of the human person' but also of what it would be for such a being to live a worthwhile life. But a worthwhile life is a good life, so how can we have a prior understanding of a good life, i.e. prior to knowing what has intrinsic value? So, I think, the best that we can likely do is to reflect on whatever is proposed as having intrinsic value and do our best to carry out the isolation test, difficult as that inevitably is.

In so far as some particular friendship has good consequences, we can say that it is a good friendship. Of course, this sense of 'good friendship' is different from a more common usage of that term: we often mean by 'good friend' a 'close friend.' Often, I think, those that we think of as good friends in one sense of the term are also good friends in the other sense of the term, but the two can come apart: I may really enjoy spending time with, say, Sally, but not feel as close to her as I feel to Linus or to Lucy. Similarly, I might be very close to Linus but, because Linus is often depressed, not always enjoy spending time with him. Or perhaps Linus is quite ill, so is not well placed to provide much in the way of emotional comfort or support to me. So the most instrumentally valuable friendships may not be the closest friendships, and vice versa.

On the other hand, it is probably more likely that if by 'good friendship' we mean to be talking about an intrinsically good friendship, then this sense of good friendship will overlap with our notion of 'good friend' in the sense of a 'close friend.' Close friends are ones with whom we are particularly intimate and with whom there is the most mutual concern; in other words, the components of the friendship relation are exemplified in a close friendship to a greater degree than in a less close one, and it is plausible to think that the greater the intimacy and concern, the greater the intrinsic value of friendship. After all, if friendship is intrinsically valuable, then that value is in some way determined by the value of the components.[1] So it is plausible to think that a closer friendship – in the sense of a more deeply caring and intimate friendship – is a more intrinsically valuable one than a less close friendship.

4.1.2 Subjective vs objective value

In discussions of value, one will often hear the claim, "Well, that might be good for you, but that doesn't mean that it is good for me." This claim is ambiguous as it stands. One potential reading of it is the following: that, say, friendship might have good consequences for you, but that does not mean that friendship will or would have good consequences for me. We can imagine Herman saying that to you after you insist to him that he is missing out on something good in not having friends in his life. And this is something that is always important to keep in mind: for anything such as friendship, its good consequences will always be contingent upon its circumstances, in particular upon the nature of the parties to the friendship and upon the other circumstances of their lives.

But there is another reading of the claim, a reading according to which something's intrinsic value is always a relative matter, determined by an individual's subjective attitudes toward the relevant thing. Thus, the claim can be read as an endorsement of what I will call 'value subjectivism':

> **Value subjectivism:** X is intrinsically good for person Y if and only if Y has the appropriate subjective attitude toward X.

What is the appropriate subjective attitude? There are a variety of suggestions that philosophers advocating value subjectivism have made, but the one that we will consider is that of desiring or wanting X intrinsically, i.e. desiring or wanting X for its own sake and not merely in virtue of its consequences. According to such a view, then, friendship is good for Herman if and only if Herman desires intrinsically that he have friends. So if Herman does not desire friends intrinsically but I do, then friendship is intrinsically good for me but not for Herman. In section 4.3 we will consider the value of friendship according to a version of value subjectivism where the appropriate subjective attitude is desiring intrinsically.

Finally, we need to consider whether friendship is objectively intrinsically valuable (section 4.4), where we are understanding objective value according to:

> **Value objectivism:** To say that X has objective intrinsic value is to say that X has intrinsic value regardless of anyone's subjective attitudes toward X.[2]

If friendship has objective intrinsic value then, regardless of Herman's attitudes toward friendship, i.e. regardless of whether Herman wants, values, or approves of friendship, his having friends would be good for its own sake. Of course, we can notice that even if friendship has objective intrinsic value, if Herman has only negative attitudes toward it, it will probably not be as instrumentally valuable in his life as it would be in the life of someone who values and approves of friendship. For example, if Herman dislikes having friends, he is likely to derive far less pleasure from having them than would someone who values having friends. Similarly, Herman's negative attitudes may make it more difficult for him to derive self-knowledge and self-improvement from his interactions with them. His attitudes will certainly make it more difficult for him to sustain any friendships that he manages to form.

In the following sections I will consider three options. First, in section 4.2 I will consider the instrumental value of friendship, in particular with respect to the consequences of pleasure, self-knowledge, and self-development. Second, in section 4.3, I will consider friendship as intrinsically valuable according to one version of value subjectivism, a version according to which the relevant subjective attitude for determining whether some X is valuable for a person Y is Y's intrinsic desiring. Third, in section 4.4, I will consider friendship as objectively intrinsically valuable, i.e. as valuable regardless of anyone's subjective attitudes toward it. Finally, in sections 4.5 and 4.6, I will consider friendship's contribution to the moral life and its role in rational deliberation.

4.2 THE CONSEQUENCES OF FRIENDSHIP

4.2.1 Pleasure

Pleasure (or at least certain pleasures) has long been regarded as having intrinsic value, i.e. as being good for its own sake. After all, when we ask someone why some X, be it money, vacations, career success, development of talents, sex, a new car, or a summer home, is worth having, the answer often takes the form, "Because I will enjoy it," or, "Because it will get me Y and I will enjoy Y." However, if we push the issue and ask, "OK, but why do you want pleasure, or to enjoy yourself?" we are likely to get a puzzled look. It seems that if you know what pleasure is, you know why it is worth having: just because of what it is, considered in and of itself.

Some philosophers have advocated Hedonism as a theory of intrinsic value:

> **Hedonism:** All and only pleasure has intrinsic value, and all and only pain is intrinsically bad.

Hedonism is a monistic account of value: it holds that one and only one type of thing, namely pleasure, has intrinsic value. We do not, however, have to accept Hedonism in order to accept that pleasure is *one* of the types of things that has intrinsic value. We can accept a pluralistic account of value, according to which pleasure is one of several or many types of things that has intrinsic value. One reason to accept that pleasure is at least one of the things that has intrinsic value is the following thought experiment: imagine a world in which you have all of the things (other than pleasure) that you take to have intrinsic value. Now change that world in just one respect: you come to enjoy or take pleasure in all of those other intrinsically valuable elements of your life. Surely your life is now even better than it was before.

There are, as with any significant philosophical issue, plenty of questions that would need to be addressed in order to defend the claim that pleasure is intrinsically valuable, most importantly, 'What is pleasure?' But, given our scope, we will set those issues aside and simply consider how friendship contributes to a pleasurable life. After all, a further, important reason for thinking that pleasure is intrinsically valuable is a consideration that I raised in Chapter One: it is, I think, very difficult to describe someone as living a happy life if she is not enjoying or taking pleasure from her life. So if we are inclined to think that the maximally valuable life would have to be a happy life, then we have reason to regard pleasure as one of the intrinsic goods composing that maximally valuable life.

Before considering the pleasures of friendship, it is important to see that even if the only reason for pursuing friendship was that it produced pleasure (in other words, even if friendship were not good for its own sake but only good in so far as it produced pleasure), it would not follow that we ought to pursue only friendships for advantage, the advantage in question being pleasure or something else such as fame or money that can bring us pleasure. In such a friendship, each party to the relationship cares about the other only as means to her own pleasure. However, in accepting the claim that pleasure is intrinsically good (or even the claim that only pleasure is intrinsically good), one is not committed to the claim that one ought to aim directly at pleasure. In fact, aiming directly at pleasure may not be the best or even one possible way of achieving pleasure. In fact, it often seems that in so far as we have only our own pleasure in sight, we are less likely to achieve it than if we had some other goal in mind. Consider something as simple as a game of bowling. It seems that the person who gets most pleasure from bowling is the person who takes as her goal the cultivation of the skills requisite to being a good bowler. Similarly, the person who engages in sexual activities with another person will often get the most pleasure from doing so if she takes the other person's pleasure as an intrinsic goal. So we cannot assume that even a Hedonist would recommend that we take our own pleasure as an intrinsic goal, i.e. as something that we aim at for its own sake.[3] Just as the one getting the most pleasure from sex or bowling is the one not focused directly on the getting of pleasure, so the friend who gets the most pleasure may not be the one who in cultivating and maintaining friendships aims only at her own pleasure.

Further, if friendship is what gives us pleasure, and friendship involves caring for another person for her own sake, then in order to get pleasure we would need to care about the other person for her own sake. If we only cared about our own pleasure for its own sake, then we could not have friends in so far as having a friend requires caring for that friend for her own sake. So it would seem that to have the instrumental good of friendship that we would have to care about something other than the consequences of friendship for its own sake, in so far as caring for another person is requisite for friendship.

So, what are the pleasures of friendship? To begin with, there are the obvious ones: we enjoy spending time with friends and engaging in various activities with them. Chatting with friends, sharing news of our lives, going to movies together, sharing a round of golf, doing chores and running errands together, telling each other jokes – these are all ways that we spend time with friends, and we choose to do them with friends because we think that we will enjoy them more that way. Tasks that are otherwise tedious or even painful become less so when we have a friend with us: painting the deck or the walls, cleaning out the garage, traveling a long distance by car or plane, grading exams – all become, even if not enjoyable, at least less painful in the company of someone we like.

But the pleasures of friendship are deeper and more significant than just having someone to help us paint the deck or to accompany us to the movies. Although it is certainly not a necessary feature of human beings, I think that it is a very common feature of us that we want to have someone understand and accept us. Modern life is stressful and requires interaction with many people on a daily basis. With most of these people, we are required to put up a front: we conform to the norms of polite interaction and we expect others to do the same. In the workplace we are required to conform to professional standards dictated by our jobs. But conforming to these norms is often a strain: doing so requires us to suppress important parts of ourselves or at least to put them aside. In fact, in some cases, we have to actually put up a false front, appearing, for example, as the boss wants, so that we keep our jobs or remain eligible for a promotion or a raise. With friends, however, we can let down our guard, as it were, and 'be ourselves,' not having to constantly self-censor or weigh how each remark will be taken by the other.

Cocking and Kennett emphasized that friends will take each other's interests as providing them with reasons to act in various ways. Thus, in friendship, we find someone who is responsive to our concerns in a positive way. Each of us will respond to the other's interpretation of her, and it is certainly pleasurable to have someone change in response to our input. As we change through the friendship, we will draw together, thereby creating a situation in which we get even more pleasure from our interactions with one another. Friends guide each other in subtle and not-so-subtle ways, and one great pleasure of at least some friendships is looking back at the ways in which you and your friend have shaped each other.

Friends know each other in special ways, and this knowledge enhances their desires to spend time with one another. Friends are often 'on the same wavelength,' as it were: they can communicate in special ways and share private jokes. Intimacy provides a space away from the fronts of daily life with strangers and mere acquaintances, a space where we can express those aspects of our identity that we take to be most central to our self-conceptions. This does not mean that we will remain static within the friendship: our interactions with our friends change us (and them) in important ways, but in ways that are likely to lead to greater pleasure for both of us. We develop shared interests and concerns, we can be together without stress or second guessing, and we have a source of care and affection that does not depend upon our conforming to societal standards. Friendship is a space that provides safety, comfort, and shared joys.

But we always have to keep in mind the drawbacks and risks of friendship. If we choose unwisely, the shaping and interpretation that is often a part of the interaction between friends will turn out to be a dangerous proposition. Take, for example, what can happen if one is impressionable and less than strong-willed. If one enters into a friendship with some- one who has bad judgment, that friendship will pose many risks. That friend's interpretation of one will often be wide of the mark, and being shaped by them could lead to diffi- culties for one in the long run – this often happens to young people when they 'get in with the wrong crowd,' as it were. The friendship itself might still be a source of pleasure but it might lead to a diminution in other sources of pleasure. The shaping that occurs in friendship might lead to great plea- sure but, if one has the 'wrong' kinds of friends, it could also lead to great pain or to a loss in other pleasures. As we de- velop a deep concern for and knowledge of another person, we can find ourselves drawn into conflicts and dilemmas. In the film *The Third Man*, Holly Martins is an intimate friend of Harry Lime. So when Holly finds out that Harry is amoral and engaged in activities that are harming and even killing innocent children (Harry is selling ineffective medications), he finds himself in a very painful situation: he must either refuse to act on the demands of justice or betray his friend to the authorities.

What these kinds of cases demonstrate is that, if we place no moral constraints on who is apt for friendship, those of us who nonetheless take our moral demands seriously can find ourselves in tricky situations. We can come to care about people who are immoral or who are just weak or have bad judgment. Our concern for them can result in the need for painful choices, and friendship with them can lead us to be worse people than we would have been without the friendship. This, of course, was the upshot of the example of Carl and Dave from the movie *Death in Brunswick* used by Cocking and Kennett (see Chapter Two).

Finally, we always have to remember the great potential that any caring relationship has to cause us pain. Many writers stress how friends (and other loved ones) expand our opportunities for pleasure, because we take pleasure in their successes and joys just as we take pleasure in our own. But the flip side is that friendship also expands our opportunities for pain, because we take pain in our friends' failures and disappointments. Further, given the great pleasure we often get from friendship, the loss of our friend through illness or death is that much more painful. The awful truth is that how the balance of pleasure over pain comes out depends upon the nature of the particular friendship. But, of course, this is true of just about any relationships or projects that we human beings might undertake. And if we take too much caution in trying to calculate how much pleasure over pain a potential friendship will bring us, we are likely to lose many opportunities for friendship as a result of being over-calculating. The bottom line is that, when considering the pleasures of friendship, it can be a risky proposition. Most of us, however, seem to judge it a risk worth taking, probably because it strikes us that a life without friends holds out almost no hope of providing us with a good balance of pleasure over pain.

Before leaving the topic of pleasure and friendship, I want to return to consideration of Thomas's claim that an important function of friendship is the mutual moral improvement of the parties to the friendship. If being moral is itself part of living a good life, and thus caring for a friend's well-being requires caring for her moral character, then Thomas's claim would certainly be correct. Would engagement in this function of friendship diminish the pleasures to be gained from such a relationship?

Many of us, as I have already pointed out, find pleasure in 'being ourselves' with our friends: we feel no need to dissemble or to hide our true feelings. We hope for friendship to provide us with a shelter in which we can safely divulge the less praiseworthy parts of our character without needing to fear a loss of standing or of affection. When I want to bitch and moan to my friends, no matter how petty I may even recognize myself as being, it is pleasurable when my friends commiserate, rather than trying to get me to see reason. I am certainly not lauding this aspect of my character, but it is a fact about me and thus is relevant to determining what will cause me to experience pleasure. And I do not think that I am entirely alone with respect to this aspect of my character. It is usually just painful to have our friends offer moral criticism or to see them as better than ourselves.

We all know, however, that focus on short-term pleasures can often reduce the overall amount of pleasure in our lives. As Thomas points out, when friends take up the mantle of moral counselor and guide, it is much less painful to face our faults than if others had to point out our shortcomings. And it is certainly less painful than having to face faults as a result of having to deal with the disastrous consequences that would come from acting on those faults. There is great pleasure in working out a coherent conception of what is worth pursuing and what sort of character we ought to have, and then actually formulating and acting on a plan to institute that conception. Doing this will reduce our shame, regret, and frustration (all painful) over time. Having a friend with whom to engage in moral and rational reflection, to provide caring guidance and criticism, can enhance the pleasures of the reflective life and allow us to avoid many of the pains of the non-reflective life. Thus, I think, even if one is focused on the pleasure to be gained from the friendship, one cannot overlook or dismiss the moral function of friendship as advocated by Thomas.

4.2.2 Self-understanding and self-development

Life with friends, then, seems generally to be a more pleasurable life than one without friends. But if we are not Hedonists, and, thereby, monists with respect to intrinsic value, we will be forced to consider what besides pleasure has intrinsic value and the role of friendship in either promoting or hindering the production of those other goods. Here I am going to consider two other candidates for entries into the category of intrinsically good things produced by friendship: self-understanding and self-development. As with pleasure, I am not going to offer a thorough defense of the claim that these have intrinsic value, but rather am going to show how friendship has a large role in producing them. After all, even if self-understanding and self-development do not have intrinsic value, they often have instrumental value, and so, if friendship is productive of self-understanding and self-development, it will still be, at least indirectly, productive of intrinsic value and so will be instrumentally valuable.

In listing things that are good for their own sake in the *Republic*, Plato lists, alongside (harmless) pleasures, knowledge. Now, Plato certainly did not mean to include all of what we might think of as knowledge as having intrinsic value: why would anyone think that knowing how many needles are on the evergreen tree outside of my window at the moment when I am typing this sentence to be good for its own sake? It is completely implausible to suppose that knowing such a fact would make my life go better. Plato, in speaking of knowledge, was speaking about knowledge about reality, about the Forms such as the Form of Beauty. I think that if we are to take any kind of knowledge to be intrinsically valuable, a plausible candidate would be knowledge of ourselves. Knowing what I truly desire and value, what goals I take to be worth pursuing, what my virtues and vices – both moral and non-moral – are, who I love, who I despise, and how my past has led me to my present seem to be part of living a good life. It is simply, I think, difficult to judge a life well-lived if the person whose life we are judging was self-deceived about important aspects of her character and values, even if that person lived a highly pleasurable life. But even if self-knowledge does not have intrinsic value, it certainly often has a great deal of instrumental value: if one is self-deceived about one's true values and character, one is likely to make decisions that leave one frustrated and dissatisfied, one will experience confusion about one's place in the world and how one is to move forward to the future. So self-knowledge, in one way or another, seems to play a significant role in leading a good life.

And friendship clearly has an important role in producing self-knowledge. One central component of friendship relations is the special knowledge that friends have of one another, and this special knowledge that, say, Lucy has of Charlie, can and often does outstrip, in various ways, the knowledge that Charlie has about himself: she might point out to Charlie that she can see that he is lonely in spite of his devotion to his work at the CDC, or that he still feels guilty about that epidemic that took him longer than usual to stem. Sally, a friend of Lucy's, might point out to her that her real reason for trying to show Charlie that he is lonely is not primarily or at least only a concern about Charlie, but rather Lucy's desire to get closer to and to spend more time with Charlie. We learn about ourselves through our friends' readings and interpretations of us.

Just as Thomas pointed out that friends can provide a safer, more comfortable way to achieve moral improvement, so also can they provide a safer, more comfortable way to achieve self-knowledge (which is itself a prerequisite of the kind of reflection required for moral improvement). Self-deception is so common precisely because understanding ourselves can be painful, but friends will provide their readings of us in a context of concern and love. And when friends tell us some home truth, they are showing us that we can be loved and accepted even once that ugly fact about us is brought into the light. Our friend continues to love us even in light of what we have been trying to avoid facing about ourselves, and this can allow us to face up to the truth ourselves.

Further, it is often true that our friends love us precisely *because*, not *in spite of*, certain features of ourselves that we do not like. Luke may not fully acknowledge just how sarcastic he can be because at some level he does not wish to be a person who is cynical and jaded. Will, however, may love Luke's sarcasm because Will is confident that Luke's never-take-anything-seriously sense of humor has helped him and will continue to help him to avoid being overly serious on many an occasion. Luke, then, can come to face and to accept features of himself that he has been avoiding trying to deal with. Will's assessment of Luke's sarcasm sheds new light for Luke on an important aspect of who he is.[4]

The ways in which friendship enhances and promotes self-knowledge are also ways in which it enhances and promotes self-improvement of many sorts, including the moral self-improvement emphasized by Thomas if the parties to the friendship are morally serious and reflective. Friends provide us with support and encouragement in developing our talents and capacities. Sometimes they do this by supporting our exercise of our talents through times of trial and disappointment, and sometimes by pointing out to us that we have certain abilities that we had never realized that we had. So, for example, Samantha may take note of how easily and naturally Darren interacts with children, whereas he himself has delayed having children for fear of not being a good father. Samantha points out that in unguarded moments with children, he responds in a caring way to which children are naturally responsive and that this type of responsiveness is an important component of good parenting. Darren will then have his confidence in being able to undertake fatherhood strengthened and he will become more likely to act on his desire to have children. Or Toni may point out to Daisy that her shyness in class is not justified because, whenever Daisy manages to get herself to contribute to classroom discussion, her comments are welcomed both by other students and by the professor. This encouragement on the basis of caring observation could have the effect of bringing Daisy out of her shell and expanding her use of her intellectual capacities.

Another important way in which friends aid in self-improvement is by leading us to use various of our capacities in our interactions with them. As I pointed out in the last section, the use of our empathetic capacities is central to our caring interaction with our friends. Thus, friendship provides an arena for becoming more empathetic, and hopefully we can then deploy that enhanced empathy in our relationships with non-intimates. As Cocking and Kennett emphasize, friendship involves taking on the interests and concerns of the other at least at some level, and so friendship can lead us to new activities and commitments, ones that we might never have undertaken apart from concerned interaction with our friend. I myself only began running in graduate school because my friend wanted to undertake a regular exercise program and I wanted to spend time with her. Running then became, for many years until my joints gave way, a central and incredibly rewarding part of my life. I came to see that I had certain kinds of endurance and physical strength that I had never before conceived of myself as having, and that exercise of physical capacity and its resultant self-understanding played a large role in increasing my self-confidence in other endeavors in my life.

We need to notice at this point, however, the extent to which these good consequences of friendship, in particular self-improvement, are contingent on the nature of the friendship. In Chapter Two I argued that frenemies can be genuine friends even given the bickering and back-biting common to many frenemy-ships. Frenemies can bring out our worst qualities, such as pettiness, jealousy, and a need to diminish others in order to feel better about ourselves. When these sorts of qualities are active in a friendship, rather than the parties coming to know themselves better and developing their capacities, they are likely to act in ways that enhance their own self-deceptions in order to give the lie to their friends' criticisms. So, in examining the potential good consequences of friendship, we always need to keep in mind how contingent those consequences are on the nature of the friends and of their bond. It is true that caring about someone involves a desire to promote that other person's well-being but, as I argued in Chapter Two, friends also have competing desires, and if friends are selfish people then their desires for their own good will often outweigh their desire for the good of the friend. Further, one might care about a friend and sincerely try to promote her good but misfire, either through lack of understanding of what is genuinely good for her or through misguided efforts to promote her good. Frenemies are often caught up in petty squabbles and so may not spend sufficient time reflecting on what their friends need and how to best help those friends to get what they need. It is just the hard truth that some friendships have very good consequences, some have very bad consequences, and some have rather middling consequences. Who we become is shaped by our friends, and so we can often read off the quality of someone's friendships by assessment of her character. Again, friendship is risky, as is just about everything.

4.3 DESIRE-SATISFACTION AND FRIENDS

4.3.1 Why do we want friends?

Many theories of well-being or intrinsic value understand a good life, at least in part, as involving getting what one wants, i.e. as involving having one's desires satisfied. We all make plans, set goals for ourselves, and our evaluation of our lives will often involve assessment of how well we are doing or have done in terms of realizing those goals. Many theories of value or well-being, however, make distinctions between desires, holding that the satisfaction of certain types of desires but not of others has intrinsic value. According to such theories, a desire must satisfy certain tests if it is to be the case that satisfying it has intrinsic value. So we can distinguish two different types of claims about the connection between desire and intrinsic value.

> **Desire-Satisfaction:** If person X intrinsically desires Y, then Y is intrinsically good for X. If person X is intrinsically averse to Y, then Y is intrinsically bad for X.

To say of someone that she intrinsically desires some Y is to say that she desires it for its own sake. So, given that I want money, but only want it as a means to other goods, I desire money not intrinsically but, rather, instrumentally: I desire it not for its own sake but only for its consequences. On the other hand, as a matter of fact, I desire my own pleasure for its own sake, and so I intrinsically desire my own pleasure and I instrumentally desire that which will bring me pleasure, such as massages, novels, tea, and chocolate. But, of course, contrary to what Thomas Hobbes claimed, most of us also intrinsically desire things other than our own pleasure: I, for example, intrinsically desire that my loved ones experience pleasure. It is certainly the case that most parents want their children to be happy and they want that for its own sake, not merely as a means to their own pleasure or happiness.

I have stated Desire-Satisfaction in such a way that it is compatible with a pluralistic account of value. So one could hold that Desire-Satisfaction is true, i.e. hold that anything that I want intrinsically has intrinsic value, and also hold that there are things that have intrinsic value (perhaps knowledge, love, and pleasure) independently of whether I (or anyone else) wants them. Or one could hold Desire-Satisfaction as a monistic theory of value, analogous to Hedonism in that respect.

Now, it seems rather obvious and not in need of extensive empirical study that most of us want to have at least one friend. But, as I have been pointing out, when thinking about why we want friends, we usually end up pointing to consequences of friendship such as pleasure. We also think of friends as providing us with stability, comfort, a safety net, etc. Some people want fame and fortune and will view friends, at least friends of a certain type, as a means of getting fame and fortune. In short, it seems to a lot of us that friends are a means to a lot of other things that we want in life, and so we have instrumental desires for friends: we see them as a means to various things that we want intrinsically. But do we have intrinsic desires for friends?

I think that the answer to this question is 'yes.' After all, even if there are other means, perhaps more efficient and less time consuming than having friends, to achieving pleasure or fame or something else, we seem to prefer that we get those other things via friendship or, at least, that friendship is one of the ways by which we acquire them. There are various explanations of why this might be the case, but one plausible explanation is that we want friendship for its own sake, not merely as a means to, for example, fame and fortune. However, there are other explanations of this claim. For example, most of us find that friends alleviate loneliness, and we do not want to experience loneliness as it is a form of psychological pain. But are there other ways of alleviating loneliness than having friends? If not, then it may be that our desires for friends are still instrumental but are unlikely to leave us, given that friends are the only means to avoid something that we desperately want to avoid.

Nonetheless, I am strongly inclined to think that many of us do have intrinsic desires for friendship understood in terms of caring intimacy. It is not implausible to suppose that at least many of us want to be close to someone for its own sake: it seems to be part of human nature to desire intimate connection. We want to have other people take our interests and concerns seriously, and this matters most to us when those other people are ones about whom we care. We want to love and be loved, and I know that I want that for its own sake, not just as a means to feeling good. After all, if I could choose between a world in which I merely believe that others love me and one in which they really do love me, I would prefer the latter world, even if the amount of pleasure in my life would be equal in the two worlds or even if the amount of pleasure in the latter world would be less. We want intimacy, love, reciprocal shaping and interpretation, and many of us, I would venture, seem to want these things for their own sake.

One important distinction to be made here is that between wanting friendship with someone or other for its own sake and intrinsically wanting a particular friendship with a particular person to continue to exist. Even if antecedent to forming any friendships I had no intrinsic desire to have friends, it is possible that once I form a friendship with Greg that I want that friendship for its own sake. My love for Greg may cause me to desire a continuing connection to him for its own sake. I think that there is plausibility to this claim: our connections to other people often seem to be components of what we regard as a life worth living, even if those connections cease to provide us with the other goods, such as pleasure, which first motivated our seeking out the friendship.[5] So, in terms of acting to acquire what we want, the forming of a friendship may be rational only in terms of what the consequences of the friendship will be, but the maintenance of the friendship may be rational in terms both of the consequences and of the friendship considered for its own sake.

4.3.2 Competent judges and their friends

Let us now return to our hermit, Herman. I have imagined that Herman has no desires for friendship: he has been there, done that, and decided that friends just are not worth the trouble. He gets no pleasure from friendship, and his solitary meditation and reflection provides him with self-understanding and use of his reflective and theoretical capacities. Unlike our example of Charlie, the CDC team leader discussed in Chapter One, Herman has not decided that he must sacrifice friendship in order to secure other goods in his life. Whereas Charlie desired friends but decided not to satisfy that desire so as to better satisfy other desires that he has, Herman does not even want friendship.

Most of us would wonder about Herman's lack of a desire for friends in his life, thinking that perhaps Herman mistook some other sort of relationship for friendship, or had friendships that were accompanied with very bad consequences and he has confused friendship itself with those consequences. Perhaps Herman is satisfied with his friendless life, but it is not always actual satisfaction that we take as a guide to how well a person's life is going. John Stuart Mill, in his work *Utilitarianism*, famously said:

> [i]t is better to be a human being dissatisfied than a pig satisfied; better to be Socrates dissatisfied than a fool satisfied. And if the fool, or the pig, is of a different opinion, it is only because they only know their own side of the question.[6]

Mill claimed that our guide to value ought to be the desires of those who are competent judges, i.e. those persons who have had a wide range of experiences of different kinds of activities and experiences. Later philosophers have followed Mill in offering some version of the following view:

> **Counterfactual Desire-Satisfaction:** If person X would intrinsically desire Y under *the relevant conditions*, then Y is intrinsically good for X. If person X would be intrinsically averse to Y under *the relevant conditions*, then Y is intrinsically bad for X.

Different versions of *Counterfactual Desire-Satisfaction* result from different characterizations of 'the relevant conditions': for Mill, the relevant conditions are those which make X a competent judge; for Richard Brandt, they are ones under which X has undergone the appropriate process of cognitive psychotherapy,[7] etc. What is important for our purposes is that *Counterfactual Desire-Satisfaction* holds that a person's actual desires are not what determines what is good for her. So even if Herman does not want friends, it might be the case that having friends would improve his life because he would want friends under the relevant conditions, e.g. perhaps Herman would want friends if he ever experienced a friendship without the negative consequences of his previous ones. Under such conditions Herman would, perhaps, be able to see the intrinsic nature of friendship because he would not have his attention and attitudes directed and shaped by the negative consequences of his previous friendships, and, in doing so, he might come to want friendship intrinsically.

As we did in discussing actual desires and friendship, it is important to make a distinction between the claim that Herman would, under the relevant conditions, want friendship with someone or other, and the claim that Herman would, under the relevant conditions, want a particular friendship with a particular person. We always have to consider the possibility that if people had sufficient information about any particular friendship they would not want it. We are forced to form friendships with less than full information about our potential friends, and it might very well be that if we knew about alternative friendships that would have been available had we passed up the ones that we had that we would not want the latter. Also, sometimes our friends turn out to be demanding or tiresome, a drain on our precious resource of time, and if we had had more information about the person we might never have sought out a friendship with her. Unless we unrealistically romanticize friendship, I do not think that it is at all plausible to suppose that it is always true that with sufficient relevant information we would always choose to make the particular friends that we have. It is perfectly consistent with the claim, "I love her," to say, "I wish that I had never met her."

I am not going to pursue the issue of friendship and *Counterfactual Desire-Satisfaction* any further because, I think, many of the reasons for imagining that someone would want friends under certain conditions are the same reasons why most of us actually want friends. However, suppose that we were to take a look at the relationships that Herman had in the past and realized that they did not have bad consequences and that they indeed counted as genuine friendships. In such a case, it is hard to say that Herman, when he decides to banish friendship from his life, is not in whatever the relevant conditions are: he has experienced genuine friendship and does not want it. Even so, I think that many of us would judge that Herman is missing something about friendship, that he is failing to see that he ought to want to have friends in his life. Perhaps friendship has objective intrinsic value, i.e. perhaps it is valuable independently of anyone's attitudes, either actual or counterfactual, with regard to it. We might, in fact, be thinking that the reason why people who do not actually desire friendship would come to desire it under the appropriate conditions is that, under those conditions, they would be able to see how objectively valuable friendship really is. So it is time to consider the objective intrinsic value of friendship.

4.4 FRIENDSHIP AS OBJECTIVELY INTRINSICALLY VALUABLE

So Herman the hermit has no friends and has no desires, either intrinsic or instrumental, to make any friends. Herman does not like people and he just wants to be left alone to meditate and contemplate reality in his desert hut. We can imagine that Herman gets a lot of pleasure from his solitary existence and would not get any pleasure from having friends. He has developed his contemplative and philosophical abilities alone in the desert, and he has come, through meditation, to have deep knowledge of himself. So it seems that Herman has been able to get the good consequences of friendship in other ways than by having friends, and having friends would not satisfy any of his actual desires. But, we might insist, surely Herman would want to have friends if he were to genuinely appreciate friendship? Surely, we think, Herman is not a competent judge: he must not have truly appreciated the friendships that he had, and so currently fails to want what he would want if he had the relevant experiences and understanding of genuine friendships.

I am inclined to think that the appropriate response to Herman is not to say, "You *would* value friendship if you really understood it," but, rather, "You *ought* to value friendship." The reason why we think that Herman would come to want friends if he truly understood genuine friendship is that, by so understanding friendship, he would come to see that it is intrinsically good just because of what it is, not because of any actual or counterfactual attitudes that he or anyone else takes with respect to it. In other words, friendship is objectively intrinsically valuable.

We need to be cautious, however, when we attempt to understand the practical implications of the claim that friendship is objectively intrinsically valuable for someone like Herman. We cannot immediately conclude from this claim that Herman, as he is, ought to incorporate friendship into his life, or even that, given his present attitudes, that it is possible for him to do so. Herman would have to change his desires, at least with respect to some particular person, if he were to have a friendship, in so far as part of what is involved in friendship is wanting to be with the other, being open to that other's needs and interests, interacting with that other in ways expressive of concern, etc. All of these seem beyond Herman's current capacities given his inclination for solitude, distaste for the company of other persons, and his failing to derive pleasure from interaction with other persons. Some intrinsic goods may be unavailable to certain persons due to their characters, personalities, inclinations, or capacities. For example, it seems fairly straightforward that psychopaths are incapable of genuine friendship in so far as they are incapable of caring for another person non-instrumentally; however, we understand what is involved in such concern: they see other people merely as tools for promoting their own interests. Similarly, some persons with severe depression suffer from anhedonia, an inability to experience pleasure, and so, if pleasure is intrinsically valuable, those with severe depression suffer from an inability to incorporate a particular intrinsic good into their lives.

We can also consider again the case of Charlie the CDC team leader from Chapter One. Charlie, we imagined, had voluntarily forgone friendship so that he would not be distracted from his life-saving work at the CDC. Charlie found solitary ways to find pleasure and to relieve stress, and his work as a team leader allowed him to develop his intellectual and leadership talents to a high degree. Even if friendship is objectively intrinsically valuable, it does not follow that Charlie ought to attempt to incorporate friendship into his life. After all, perhaps he is right in thinking that the sort of particularistic bond involved in friendship would detract from his ability to do his job, and his inability to balance his competing responsibilities would make him feel guilty and resentful. If we are pluralists about value, i.e. if we accept that more than one type of thing has intrinsic value, we have to allow for the very real possibility that we must make choices regarding which goods to include in our life plans, and such choices should be guided by facts about our temperaments, abilities, and circumstances.[8] In forgoing friendship, it is quite possible that both Charlie and Herman have made rationally and even morally justified choices. (We will consider these issues further in sections 4.5 and 4.6.)

However, we might think that friendship is different from an intrinsic good such as pleasure, for example. Perhaps friendship differs either quantitatively or in some other way from other intrinsic goods, thereby making it unlikely that a life without friendship is a good life. So let us consider such possibilities.

4.4.1 The quantitative view

Not all intrinsically valuable things are valuable to the same degree. Certainly, goods of the same type can vary in their degree of value. Pleasure, for instance, as Jeremy Bentham famously noted, varies across several dimensions, most importantly intensity and duration.[9] For example, the pleasure of sexual orgasm is very brief but extremely intense, while the pleasure of reading a novel will be more long-lived but nowhere near as intense (unless it is one hell of a novel). Bentham plausibly claimed that the value of any particular pleasure is a function of both its intensity and duration, so that the value of the pleasure of reading a novel for the same length of time as it takes to have an orgasm would be far less than the pleasure of that orgasm, although the overall pleasure of reading the novel, given its duration, may be greater than the pleasure of the orgasm.

Similarly, it seems plausible to suppose that we can compare the values of intrinsic goods of different types. For example, if I were asked to trade away my friendship with Marcy for a 5 percent overall increase in the pleasure in my life, I would refuse the trade, which suggests that I regard my friendship with Marcy as more valuable than that particular amount of pleasure.[10] In the previous section I suggested that, as long as friendship is only one component of the good, we could then make trade-offs between friendship and other intrinsic goods, and live just as good, if not better, lives without friends than we would with friends. But that claim presupposed that other goods and friendship are roughly in the same ballpark with respect to how valuable they are. Suppose, however, that friendship were really significantly more valuable than any other intrinsic good, so that, in fact, the amount of pleasure plus any other intrinsic goods other than friendship that one could fit into a single lifetime could never make that life anywhere near as valuable as friendship could make it. We can compare this to what Mill says about the relative values of higher, or intellectual, pleasures, as opposed to lower, or bodily, pleasures. Mill, holding some type of Counterfactual Desire-Satisfaction account of value, claimed that higher-quality pleasures are far more valuable than the lower-quality ones because competent judges would not trade away the higher-quality pleasures for any amount of the lower-quality pleasures. Thus, Mill was suggesting that no amount of lower-quality pleasures could compensate for the complete loss of higher-quality pleasures.[11] We might say something similar about friendship: no amount of other intrinsic goods could possibly compensate for the loss of friendship. A life without friendship might have some intrinsic value, on this view, but it would nonetheless be a greatly impoverished life.

This view does possess some plausibility in so far as we agree with the claim from Aristotle that I quoted previously: "no one would choose to live without friends even if he had all the other goods." Aristotle here seems to be saying about friendship relative to other goods what Mill was saying about higher-quality pleasures relative to lower-quality pleasures: no reasonable person would trade away the former, no matter how much of the latter she could get. And it is undoubtedly true that we often pity someone who lacks friends, even if she has all of the other intrinsic goods, thus giving further credence to the view that, with respect to degree of value, friendship is way off of the charts, as it were.

On the other hand, we can imagine cases such as that of Charlie, the CDC team leader, with respect to whom pity seems quite inappropriate. Surely Charlie is living at least as good of a life as someone with a couple of friends who has failed at all other endeavors and has no sense of purpose in his or her life. A plausible explanation of why we usually pity the friendless is because we imagine that they must be lonely, even if they will not acknowledge it. They have no one to share in their interests and whose interests to share, they do not experience deep reciprocal affection, and, we might be thinking, it does not matter if you have a yacht and five homes, that just cannot alleviate your sense of isolation in order to compensate for the loss of love. But notice that if this is what explains our intuitions then, once again, it is only friendship plus its consequences, i.e. its intrinsic plus its instrumental value, that seems to be so central to our conception of a good life. And someone like Charlie might be lonely but we have no reason to think that that loneliness cannot be more than compensated for by his meaningful work, in which he uses his talents to the fullest, and the resultant sense of purpose he experiences. So even if friendship is one of the most, or even the most, valuable of intrinsic goods, it may yet be rational for someone such as Charlie to forgo friendship.

4.4.2 Friendship and organic wholes

In order to provide friendship with an essential role in the good life, we might adopt Moore's view about organic wholes. Moore claimed that determining the value of some whole is not always the same as determining the number of pieces of fruit in a basket.[12] Each piece of fruit counts as one: add a banana to X pieces of fruit, now you have $X + 1$ pieces of fruit. Take away three kiwis from X pieces of fruit, and now you have $X - 3$ pieces of fruit. If addition of value worked the same way, then if you added three items together, X with no intrinsic value, Y with 3 units of value, and Z with 1, you would then have a state of affairs with 4 units of intrinsic value. Moore, however, claimed that there are organic wholes, i.e. wholes such that the sum of the value of their parts taken independently does not equal the value of the whole. For example, suppose that a beautiful work of art has 50 units of value, and a pleasure of a certain intensity and duration has ten units of value. One cannot, however, simply suppose that the state of affairs of my getting a pleasure of that intensity and duration by contemplating that work of art will have 60 units of value: perhaps it has more, because my getting that amount of pleasure from something of beauty renders the state of affairs more valuable than the art and the pleasure considered in isolation from each other.[13]

Thus, if we accept Moore's view about organic wholes, we could claim that, while friendship may be on a par with respect to the amount of intrinsic value it has relative to other intrinsic goods, a life which contains, say, friends, use of talents, and pleasure has more than the amount of value contained in the sum of a life with only friends, plus a life with only the use of talents, plus a life with only pleasure. Or, to make friendship essential to a good life, we could say that the presence of friendship is a necessary condition of a life's having any intrinsic value at all. So, then, a life with only pleasure and the use of talents would have no value, a life with friends but no pleasure or use of talents would have some value, and a life with friends, pleasure, and use of talents would have yet more intrinsic value. Thus, according to this view, friendship would not only be an important good, but a good that is essential to a valuable life.

However, I find the claim that nothing has value without friendship to be implausible. We do often say, for example, that a pleasure shared is better, but surely some solitary pleasures are good. Consider solitary sexual pleasure derived from thinking about a sexual fantasy that one hopes that no one else ever finds out about. Why suppose that such a pleasure would not have value in a life without friends? Or suppose that I write great novels, using my talents to produce works with a profound understanding of the human condition. Surely, it seems, my life has some value as a result of my use of my talents and my resultant accomplishments, even if my life would most likely have been better if I had had some friends with whom to share my accomplishments (although Charlie always stands as an example cautioning us not to jump too hastily to such a conclusion). We need some pretty compelling arguments, it seems, before we accept the claim that all value in a life depends on the subject of that life's having friends.

However, the claim that friendship in conjunction with, say, the use of one's talents has more value than does friendship on its own added to the use of one's talents on one's own seems more plausible. So my friendship with Richard might have a certain quantum of value and my writing of this book has some other quantum of value. But perhaps when I write the book in dialogue with Richard's input and encouragement, the amount of value is increased exponentially. This claim, I think, has some plausibility. Pursuing the other valuable aspects of my life in the context of caring, intimate relationships seems to give those other aspects added value, and perhaps also give the relationships added value. If, for example, Charlie from the CDC could do all that he does but do it in a life with friends, perhaps his life would increase in value by more than just the value of the friendships. Again, it is difficult to assess this claim because, in adding friendship, we are also likely adding various good consequences and we might be surreptitiously taking those into account in assessing the value of the resultant life. But we will return to the issue of organic wholes in Chapter Five when we consider how to assess the value of close friendships versus less-close friendships.

4.5 FRIENDSHIP, VIRTUE, AND THE GOOD LIFE

In Chapter One I discussed the connection between living a good life and being a morally good person. Let us suppose that being a morally good or virtuous person is objectively intrinsically good, and that it is an intrinsic good either far superior in value to any other good (the quantitative view) or that it is such that a life lacks value if the subject of that life is not morally good (the organic wholes view). Kant seemed to hold the latter view, saying that a good will (which we can here take to be the same as a good character) is the only unconditional good: it is the only thing that is intrinsically valuable no matter what else is true of the world.[14] All other things depend for their goodness upon the good character of the person in whose life they occur. Thus, the pleasure of a bad person is not good, while the pleasure of a morally good person is good. Plato, on the other hand, seemed to hold the first view: no other goods can compensate for the loss of virtue.[15] Thus, it is better to be a morally good person who has no other goods than to be a morally bad person who has all of the other goods.

Both Aristotle and Thomas would agree with the importance that Plato and Kant gave to a morally good character. For Aristotle, living well is living in accordance with the virtues,[16] while Thomas views being morally good as a crucial part of human flourishing. If one takes being morally good to be crucial in some way to living a good life, then adopting one of the moralized conceptions of friendship would give friendship an important, even if not necessary, place in the good life.

For both Aristotle and Thomas, friendship plays a key role in developing and/or maintaining a virtuous character. For Thomas, friends provide us with moral criticism that we are likely to take to heart, a moral example to which we are able to aspire, motivation and support in our efforts to be morally good, and space in which to develop various moral sensibilities. For Aristotle, complete friends are virtuous partners in pursuit of the good, and friendship, he believed, was also an essential arena for the exercise of certain virtues. The morally good person is, for example, generous, but while it is admirable to be generous to strangers or mere acquaintances, it is most admirable to display these qualities in our interactions with our friends.[17] Thus, to be as morally good as possible, a human being needs friends because only with friends can she exercise all of the virtues to their fullest.

Only Aristotle's view gives friends an essential role in the good life, once we assume that virtue is necessary for a good life. If there are certain virtues only available in the context of friendship,[18] then friends are necessary for complete virtue, which is itself necessary for the flourishing of the individual. Thomas's view, on the other hand, sees friendship as instrumental to the production of virtue, given certain common features of human psychology. For example, Thomas says that while "a moral person recognizes the importance of being made aware of her shortcomings, ... being made aware of them is not a source of delight for her," and neither "do we delight in others' discovering [our moral shortcomings]."[19] Thus, having a morally serious and committed friend to make it easier for us to accept criticism, and before whom we can have our flaws revealed without fear of rejection, is important to our being able to morally improve ourselves.

Of course, many people have questioned Aristotle's understanding of friendship in so far as it is only possible between fully virtuous persons. Thomas's view of friendship does not require that the parties to that kind of friendship be virtuous, but if friends are to play the role in the moral life that Thomas sees them as playing, they do need to be morally serious or, as he calls them, "morally grounded." For many if not most of us, our friends are not the sort of moral exemplars and counselors that Thomas conceives of them as being. Even if we do sometimes admire and try to emulate aspects of our friends and seek their advice, more often than not we look to them to take our minds off our troubles, to help to soothe our consciences, and to take our sides even in cases where, at least at some level, we and they both know that we were in the wrong. Sometimes we even appreciate the less-than-admirable features of our friends, looking to them for a good gossip or a session of being snarky about third parties.

But we always have to keep in mind, in our interactions with our friends, that if we care about them then one of our goals is to promote their good. It is then quite important that we attempt to determine the connection between being a morally good person and living a valuable life. If one cannot do well if one does not have some at least minimal level of moral virtue, then one will be failing to act in a concerned manner if one ignores or even encourages a friend's slide into moral vice. This does not mean that we would then have to give up having a good gossip or being snarky with a friend because, as long as being morally virtuous is not the only component of a good life, we still have to think about a friend's pleasure, etc. We just have to make sure that we do not allow our indulgences with our friends to undermine entirely their moral well-being.

Suppose, however, that being morally virtuous is not even a part of what is involved in living a good life, i.e. suppose that being morally good is not intrinsically good. If it is instrumentally good, it is more likely to produce good consequences for others than for the morally good person herself. Nonetheless, morality still provides us with reasons for action, reasons for action that have nothing to do with our own good and that may in certain circumstances outweigh the reasons to promote our own good. If those reasons arise in friendship, then regardless of the role of friendship in living a good life, we will have reasons to act to care for our friends.

4.6 FRIENDSHIP AND RATIONALITY

In Chapter Two we discussed two different accounts of the types of reasons generated by friendship. According to the account offered by Cocking and Kennett, friendship generates special non-moral reasons, while according to my own account friendship generates special moral obligations. Where both accounts agree is in accepting that what we have reason to do is at least in part a function of the demands of our friendships. Importantly, then, these accounts of friendship render it the case that friendship is relevant to what rationality requires of us. This is important because the demands of friendship may compete against other moral demands and also against the promotion of our own good.

Consider again the case of Dave and Carl. Cocking and Kennett and I agree that Dave has reasons to help Carl to hide the body. These reasons, whether we consider them moral reasons or not, compete against Dave's moral reasons to alert the police and to let the victim's family learn what has happened to their loved one. But they also compete against reasons that Dave has to promote his own good. Dave would be in serious legal trouble if the facts come to light, he could lose his job given that he desecrated a grave at the cemetery where he works, and he has surely created a lot of anxiety and stress for himself. Even if we accept that Dave's friendship with Carl is intrinsically good, it is clear that if Dave acts on his reasons to help Carl, he will be causing himself a lot of suffering as well as a further great risk of horrible suffering.

So friendship generates reasons, whether they be moral or non-moral, for action that could make it rational for us to act against our own good. Just as many people think that morality can sometimes demand that we sacrifice our own good, so it seems that these accounts of friendship and its reasons imply that rationality can sometimes demand that we sacrifice our own good. Rather than getting a picture in which friendship unequivocally makes our lives better, we end up with a picture according to which friendship may make it the case that we are required to perform actions that will make our lives far worse.

And perhaps this is not so surprising. We can understand, for example, a resistance fighter who recognizes that she may lose everything if she is caught and yet insists that her cause is important enough to her that she is willing to take the risk. We do not say in such a case that fighting for her cause makes her life go better: fighting for what matters to her may cause her great suffering. Similarly, then, it makes sense to say that friendship may cost us our well-being but that it is worth the cost in some sense. Our friends, by their very nature, matter to us. But what matters to us may demand that we act in ways detrimental to our own good.

Of course, we enter friendships generally thinking that by doing so we will improve our lives, either as an intrinsic matter or as an instrumental matter. But by coming to care about someone, we have committed to them in an important way. So friendship, we might say, is a risk: we certainly want and hope that it will contribute to our doing well but, once entered, we have reasons to act in ways that may undermine our doing well. There is a very important truth to what all of our parents constantly said to us: "Don't get mixed up with the wrong crowd." The problem, of course, is that we do not always know in advance who counts as the 'wrong crowd,' and who belongs in that category may be a matter of circumstance as much as a matter of character. Tony may have been a charming, helpful friend to Carole if he had not gotten cancer and thereby demanded great care, and eventually caused terrible grief and loss for her when he died a painful death. But given the potentially great benefits of friendship, both in and of itself and in virtue of its consequences, for most of us it seems that it is irrational not to take the risk that is friendship.

NOTES

1 We will see, however, in section 4.4.2 that the way in which the value of the whole is determined by the value of the components or parts may not be a straightforward matter.

2 Some readers will have noticed that I have tried to state value subjectivism and value objectivism as neutral between a meta-ethical and a normative reading, i.e. as neutral between offering a conception of what value is and offering a conception of what has value. Value subjectivism can be understood as a meta-ethical claim, according to which what it is for something to have value for a given person is for it to be the object of that person's relevant attitude (be it desiring, valuing, approving, etc.). But it can also be understood as a normative claim about what types of states of affairs have intrinsic value, i.e. as stating that states

that constitute or involve the satisfaction of desire have intrinsic value. For our purposes, this important distinction is not relevant, so I leave it aside in the main text.

3 This is related to the so-called 'paradox of Hedonism.' See Joseph Butler's classic discussion in his *Fifteen Sermons Preached at the Rolls Chapel*, reprinted in D. D. Raphael (ed.), *British Moralists 1650–1800* (Indianapolis, IN: Hackett Publishing, 1991): 334.

4 See also Cocking and Kennett, "Friendship and Moral Danger": 286.

5 As Nehamas puts it, "We can never be sure that friendship, however genuine, guarantees that we will end up better off than we were before we met" (*On Friendship*: 198). Nehamas presents a view concerning friendship and the good life very similar to the view presented here, but in a more literary rather than analytical mode. My point here is that the friendship itself, stripped of its contingent consequences, may still be something that we want for its own sake and, thus, still a contributor of value to our lives.

6 John Stuart Mill, *Utilitarianism* (Indianapolis, IN: Hackett Publishing, 1979): 10.

7 Richard Brandt, *A Theory of the Right and the Good* (New York, NY: Oxford University Press, 1979).

8 We can see here a way in which an intrinsically valuable life might not be a happy life. We can imagine someone with lots of friends and accomplishments who suffers from a melancholy disposition and so does not take pleasure in her intimate connections or in her accomplishments. If both friendship and accomplishment in the sense of development and deployment of talents are both objectively intrinsically valuable, then such a person would be living a valuable life but not a happy life. Such a person might not even be capable of leading a happy life.

9 Jeremy Bentham, *The Principles of Morals and Legislation* (New York, NY: Hafner Press, 1948): 29–32.

10 Matters are more complicated than this. Perhaps I am covertly considering the various consequences of friendship along with friendship when I weigh its value against the reduction in pleasure. If so, then all that I would be able to conclude is that it seems that friendship in conjunction with its various consequences is more valuable than a certain quantum of pleasure. This illustrates one of the difficulties with carrying out the isolation test. All that we can do is attempt as best we can to think about friendship in isolation from its standard or expected consequences.

11 *Utilitarianism*: 8–11. For an excellent discussion of Mill on the higher pleasures, see David O. Brink, *Mill's Progressive Principles* (Oxford: Oxford University Press, 2013), Chapter 3.

12 In *Principia Ethica*, Thomas Baldwin (ed.) (Cambridge: Cambridge University Press, 1993 [1903]), 78–87. Moore defines organic wholes as being such that "the value of such a whole bears no regular proportion to the sum of the value of its parts" (79).

13 Of course, organic wholes could work in such a way that the addition of some particular type of good, in certain circumstances, actually decreases the value of the whole. So, for example, someone might hold that pleasure is intrinsically valuable and pain is intrinsically bad. Suppose that one has a pleasure of ten units and a pain of ten units. Instead of the resulting complex having 0 units of value, it might be said that the complex has some amount of value less than zero if the pleasure is pleasure resulting from the pain of another person.

14 In *Grounding for the Metaphysics of Morals*: 7–8.

15 I take it that Plato must hold this view if he is to have an adequate response to Glaucon's example of the perfectly just man versus the perfectly unjust man (*Republic*: 360e–362c).

16 Aristotle has a conception of the virtues that extends beyond our narrower conception of moral virtues. However, for our purposes here what matters is that Aristotle includes what we would regard as the moral virtues among the virtues.

17 *Nichomachean Ethics*: 1169b10–15.

18 Thomas could similarly hold that certain moral sensibilities are only appropriate in relation to friends, rather than saying that friendship merely provides an arena for developing moral sensibilities important to the moral life as a whole. Taking the former line would allow Thomas, like Aristotle, to see friendship as essential to the best life for a human being.

19 *Living Morally*: 141.

Five

Friendship makes our lives go better in multiple ways. It produces good consequences such as pleasure, self-knowledge, and self-development, it satisfies both intrinsic and instrumental desires that most of us have, and, plausibly, it is intrinsically valuable. But does friendship contribute value to our lives in the same ways or to the same extent if it is maintained via social media? Can social media usage hinder the production of the standard good consequences of friendship? Can it reduce the intrinsic value of friendship? In using social media, are we gaining the advantages of convenience in keeping in touch with friends and of maintaining friendships over great distances, but reducing or even losing the value of friendship in our lives? Are we in some sense trading quantity (our multitude of Facebook 'friends') for quality?

These are complicated questions, the answers to which require input from researchers from a range of disciplines, in particular sociology and psychology. My goal in this chapter is to show how our philosophical examination of the nature of friendship and the nature of the good life can reveal to us the ways in which social media threatens to reduce friendship's contribution to the good life. I will give some attention to empirical research carried out in those other disciplines, but the studies that have been carried out have limitations. In particular, a lot of research has focused on the consequences of social media usage for relationships among young people, in particular among adolescents. But friendships between teenagers are quite different from adult friendships, just as the capacity of teenagers to live intrinsically good lives is quite different from that of mature adults. Also, it is likely that adults use social media differently from the ways in which adolescents use it. Nonetheless, the empirical research that has been done does tend to reinforce the claims that I will make about the dangers of social media usage.

I also think that one important role of the philosopher is to suggest future directions that empirical research can take. Philosophers, in analyzing concepts, show connections, such as the connections that we examined in the previous chapter between friendship and the good life. In doing so, we can then locate possible ways in which those connections can be broken by, for example, social media usage in friendship. The potential obstacles to maintaining the value in our lives that friendship contributes in the light of Facebook, texting, and Twitter, which I will point out in this chapter, can then be explored by social scientists. It is also the case that if social scientists are to explore how social media usage affects the value of friendship, they need to understand the concepts of friendship and of value so that they can correctly locate in real life that which they are attempting to study. So what we discuss in this chapter, in combination with the conceptual analyses of Chapters Two and Four, can provide guidance for future empirical research on the effects of social media on friendship and the good life.

The features of social media that pose a challenge to maintaining valuable relationships are also those features that have been heralded as social media's advantages: the ways in which social media allows us to connect to more people, to connect to those people no matter where we are or what we are doing, to control how, when, and whether we choose to respond to 'friends,' and to 'block,' quite easily, those with whom we are upset, offended, or angry for one reason or another. Perhaps surprisingly, the ability to connect to more people more often seems to enhance loneliness and isolation, two unpleasant states that we standardly think of friendship as preventing or at least alleviating. I will argue that by examining the nature of loneliness we can see why this fact is not at all surprising, and I will re-emphasize the importance of face-to-face and one-on-one contact with friends.

Although I will focus on the dangers that social media poses to the value of friendship, I do not intend this chapter to be any sort of thorough-going indictment of social media usage in friendship. I have emphasized throughout this book that we cannot formulate any interesting necessary truths about friendships making our lives better or worse. So we need to keep in mind that there are as many ways of using social media in a friendship as there are friendships. My goal, then, is to show how and where we need to be careful when we use social media in our friendships so that we do not reduce the value, either instrumental or intrinsic, of those relationships, and thereby reduce the value of our own lives and of the lives of those we care about.

5.1 GETTING GOOD RESULTS ON FACEBOOK

5.1.1 The pleasures of trust, openness, and private space

One obvious good consequence of friendship, as we discussed in Chapter Four, is pleasure: friendship can and often does bring us great joy. We enjoy spending time with our friends and they can alleviate the pains of loneliness, depression, failure, and anxiety. Friends support us in difficult times and share the good times, thereby making those good times even more enjoyable.

An important basis of the pleasure that we derive from friendship is the trust that standardly exists in such a relationship. Friends, at least friends of long standing, usually trust one another to be open and honest with one another and, reciprocally, to not betray revelations and disclosures to third parties. This trust and openness creates an atmosphere of understanding and acceptance where friends can 'be themselves' without the constraints of formal social interactions, such as the rules of etiquette, politeness, and professionalism. It also allows for a space in which criticism, in particular moral criticism, can be offered without superiority and smug judgment on the one side or defensiveness and offense on the other. Thus, friends can move us toward self-knowledge and self-improvement in a way that can even make such endeavors fun rather than ridden with shame and feelings of inadequacy. So trust, openness, and creation of a private space free from the constraints of, for example, the workplace or formal social gatherings are crucial to the production of some of the primary consequences of friendship, namely pleasure, self-development or self-improvement, and self-knowledge.

But social media is not well-suited to building, reinforcing, or maintaining trust, openness, or private space, or, at least, the most commonly used aspects of social media are not well-suited to doing so. As I emphasized (and as many of the philosophical commentators on social media and friendship, in particular Cocking and Matthews,[1] have emphasized) we have a great deal of control over how we present ourselves on social media. Most of us present the 'greatest hits' of our lives, as it were: we choose the great-looking vacations, the happy (or happy-looking) times with our families, the drinks with friends, the new car, etc. There are many reasons why we do this, but surely one is that our Facebook pages are open and available to more than our closest circle of intimates: no one, after all, has over 100 close, intimate friends, but most people do, in fact, have over 100 Facebook 'friends.' But then it seems that we are editing our lives for semi-public consumption, with making ourselves appear enviable, or at least interesting and attractive, one of the primary motivators of what we share.

Numerous studies have been done about the links between Facebook, envy, and depression.[2] While the studies sometimes have conflicting results, they do appear to confirm links between Facebook and envy, and, as a result, links between Facebook and depression. Facebook, it seems, leads to constant comparison between one's own life and the lives of one's 'friends.' And because the vast majority of us post only our 'greatest hits,' when we look at our friends' pages, their lives look amazing: great vacations, happy families, lots of good times with good friends, etc. While we also have posted the images and comments that present our own lives in the best light possible, we are, obviously, inevitably deeply entrenched in the messy entirety of our own lives, and so are fully aware of our careful curating of our own lives for social media presentation and consumption. We then compare the entirety of our own lives with only the best of our friends' lives and, not surprisingly, our own lives come up far short. Thus, we feel inadequate and unhappy: why can't we have one of those perfect lives that everyone else has?[3]

What impact can this comparison-induced envy and depression have on friendship? Here we can only speculate, given the lack of detailed studies. However, it seems quite obvious that the conditions present on social media are not ripe for the creation of openness and trust. Friendship requires that I share enough of myself with another person that she can get a picture of who I am, both with respect to my strengths and with respect to my weaknesses. Trust builds as we recognize that the other has not betrayed what we shared in confidence, nor told third parties about our embarrassing moments or about our failures. We also develop trust in another when we recognize that they have seen some unattractive features of our characters and personalities, and are still, for whatever reason, sticking around and exhibiting care and love for us. If, however, we feel compelled to try to present only the positive aspects of ourselves and of our lives, we are not giving our friends the material that they need to see us as whole people. We are withholding that which we fear will be judged in a negative manner because we already feel bad enough about ourselves when we are only posting the positive. So we provide nothing about ourselves which, in being kept private, can form a basis for trust to develop: everything posted is already available to tens or even hundreds of people and, given the positive nature of what we have posted, we are not reassured of being loved, warts and all.

Further, the most used features of social media such as Facebook are the semi-public, not the one-on-one features. This means that posts are directed at an audience rather than at any particular individual person. In so far as we reveal different aspects of ourselves to different friends, when we edit our lives for all of our friends at once we tend to present the 'common denominator' of ourselves, as it were. In other words, we are less open about how we feel, what we are doing, and what is happening to us than we would be in one-on-one interaction, be it face-to-face or not. We share only that which we would be willing to share, no matter which one of our friends we were interacting with. Thus, much that sustains the unique bond of each particular friendship gets edited away.[4]

The results of the lessened trust and openness that are characteristic of more traditional friendships is the reduction of our ability to create a private space free from the formal constraints of, for example, professionalism and politeness. We have to maintain a guard on social media that prevents us from being wholly ourselves, where, as we discussed in Chapter Four, the ability to be ourselves with our friends is one of the most important ways in which friendship gives us pleasure. And here, I think, one of the aspects of online interaction which we noted Briggle as praising (Chapter Three) – namely the ability to weigh and assess what we post, to be more deliberate in what we say – can be seen to potentially diminish one of friendship's joys: the spontaneity and openness of give-and-take between friends. This kind of spontaneity allows us to avoid thinking through what we 'ought' to be saying and to avoid always considering how we will appear: we can just be in the moment, revealing ourselves with the ability to immediately see the other's interpretations and misinterpretations of us and to immediately respond to those interpretations and misinterpretations. Briggle is right to see the online world as providing a buffer between us and those with whom we are communicating but, I think, many of the pleasures of friendship come from not employing or even feeling the need to have such a buffer. While such a buffer may allow some kinds of interaction to get off of the ground that would not have done so otherwise, I think that in established friendships they can reduce the sources of pleasure.

5.1.2 Social media, loneliness, and isolation

As I said in the introduction to this chapter, there seems to be some evidence that, at least for some people, social media is actually enhancing, rather than reducing, their loneliness and sense of isolation.[5] Facebook is heralded as a way for us to maintain and enhance connection, to have wider connections, and, thus, to be less isolated. So why is it, at least for some of us, working in just the opposite way? What might explain a link between Facebook and loneliness and feelings of isolation?

I think that if we are to answer this question, we need to have some understanding of the nature of loneliness. We all know that being alone is neither necessary nor sufficient for loneliness. For all of us, there are times at which we enjoy our solitude, and there are people (I myself am one of them) who need a great deal of solitude in order to be content with their lives. At such times, which come more or less often depending on the individual, being alone is not accompanied by loneliness, which is by its nature a painful state; rather, at such times, our solitude gives us pleasure by, for example, allowing peace and quiet for reflection or rest, giving us space to read or write without disruption or distraction, offering an opportunity to just completely 'let our hair down,' etc. On the other hand, we also know that we can at times be with other people, either one-on-one or in a small or large group, and feel intense loneliness. I know that I have sometimes felt the most agonizing loneliness when I am at large social gatherings, and that the feeling of loneliness actually only dissipates when I am alone at home once more.

We could engage in quite abstract, existential musings about why human beings experience loneliness. However, I think that, given that the pains of loneliness are not correlated with the presence or absence of other persons, and yet have something to do with our existence relative to that of others, there is a quite commonsense explanation of what the feeling of loneliness amounts to: it is a feeling that arises from a sense, feeling, or belief that we do not have the types of connections to other persons, be they present or not, that we want or think that it would be desirable to have. Thus, it is not uncommon, in my own case, for my feelings of loneliness to come to the fore when I am in large social gatherings. I feel isolation because I do not feel sufficiently attached to any one person: I feel left out in some sense, even if I carry on a succession of conversations with other party-goers. The conversations at such gatherings tend to be 'small talk,' and I feel the need to make sure that I make what will be perceived as the appropriate responses so as not to offend in any way. I do not discuss what really matters to me because I do not feel that the other person cares sufficiently about me to take an interest or to respond in a helpful manner. So each successive conversation appears fungible to an extent, and I myself feel somewhat like a placeholder. I also feel pressure to be interesting or amusing, and feel constantly judged as to how I am performing according to those standards.

If a lack of desired or desirable connection is what causes the pain of loneliness, then it becomes quite clear why the presence of a friend but not of a stranger or a mere acquaintance is its required remedy. We saw in the previous section that friendship creates, via trust and openness, a private space for two people where they can be themselves and interact in ways that express, and are recognized as expressing, concern. Thus, ideally, in the space created by friendship, each party feels that she matters to the other, that her concerns are taken seriously, and pretense and constraint can be dropped without fear. This is the kind of connection to another person that most of us desire in desiring friendship, and it is its absence or perceived absence that causes us to feel lonely.[6]

Given the nature of loneliness and feelings of isolation, why might social media not be well-suited to alleviating them? The discussion in the last section has already provided us with the answer: social media is not suited to creating the type of private space that is built on openness and trust. When we log on to a friend's Facebook page, we see that she has 112 friends, has gone out for drinks with some friends (not including us), has taken a great vacation with her partner, etc. Many of her 112 friends have liked her photos and videos, telling her how great she is and how much they love her. She has posted some political comments with which you disagree, but you do not feel comfortable adding a dissenting voice to all of the comments that have seconded your friend's viewpoint. Your friend's posts are not meant just for you and, as we discussed in the previous section, have, in many cases, been crafted in order to present a certain image, a desirable persona. What you are often presented with are images of your friend doing a lot of things that do not include you. So your intimate connection is swamped in the presentation meant for semi-public consumption.

It seems that no matter how wonderful an activity you might be involved with – say, a romantic getaway in Paris – that logging on to Facebook can cause you to enjoy it less. You will log on and see what your friends are doing together in your absence – perhaps something as mundane as cheap beers at a dive bar – and this will cause you to feel left out and, thereby, less involved in and less happy with your day at the Louvre with your partner. Seeing what your friends are doing without you causes a feeling of isolation.[7] Of course, prior to Facebook we all knew that our friends continued to exist and to do things in our absence, but we did not have the means to wallow in and dwell on it. Now, it seems, even when we have available the appropriate sort of meaningful connection to the person who we are with, we still feel lonely because we are focusing on what we feel is an absence or attenuation of some other meaningful connection.

Another feature of Facebook and Twitter that can, I believe, cause feelings of isolation and loneliness is the fact that we are completely free to choose when and even whether we respond. Some people like this feature of social media and of texting because they do not feel the pressure to respond immediately. They can also ignore a text or posting if they like. However, we all know how we can feel if we are not the ones ignoring a text or a post but the one having a text or post ignored.[8] Because we think that everyone has her smartphone or tablet with her at all times, too long of a delay in getting a response to a text or a post suggests to us that our friend is ignoring or deprioritizing us. The ease of using technology to keep in touch has the downside of making us wonder why our friends aren't keeping in better touch with us: if it is so easy and they are not doing it, what does that say about their attitude toward us?

Finally, we need to recall that one of the greatest pleasures of friendship is just spending time with our friends. But in our busy lives, we need to make space and exert effort to actually get together with friends. Now, however, we have the option to chat online, check each other's Facebook pages, text, etc. Having done those things we might, and, I think, many of us do, decide that we have done what we need to do to maintain the friendship, to keep in touch and up-to-date with our friend, and thus we make less effort to meet up face-to-face. Recall, however, the quotation from Sharon Vallor that I cited in Chapter Three:

> I might speak of "maintaining" my garden, when by this I mean throwing enough water on it just often enough to keep it limping along, or I might refer to my sustained and careful efforts to nourish and tend to it lovingly, to ensure that every part of it not only lives, but thrives.

Hanging out with friends is one of the great pleasures of having them, and if we convince ourselves that we can just as easily maintain the friendship without doing so, we thereby lose one of the most enjoyable consequences of friendship and, we will see in the following sections, most likely also reduce friendship's intrinsic value.

5.1.3 Knowledge and improvement online

Our discussion in Chapter Three about how the special knowledge that is often a component of the intimacy characteristic of friendship can be diminished via online interactions is also relevant to a discussion of how social media usage can diminish the instrumental value of friendship. One of the good consequences of friendship that we discussed in Chapter Four is self-knowledge: interaction with friends can lead us to understand ourselves better, and this self-knowledge is key to improvement and development, particularly moral development. Friends can read us, and they are perceptive with respect to our behavior and feelings because they interact with us in caring ways. However, as we saw in Chapter Three, the lack of face-to-face interaction can diminish friends' empathetic capacities with respect to one another in so far as important bodily cues and modes of expression are filtered out when we interact on Facebook. Then friends do not have the same quality of special knowledge with respect to each other, and so are in a less privileged position with respect to leading each other to self-knowledge.

Probably the biggest obstacle to friends leading each other to self-knowledge is the fact, emphasized by Cocking and Matthews, that we have significantly greater control over how we present ourselves online as compared to how we present ourselves in face-to-face interaction. By filtering out the negative and picking only the positive for the semi-public arena of a Facebook page, we prevent our friends from getting to know us in a way that then allows them to interpret us in a meaningful and robust manner. My friend can only respond to what I post, and so it is far more difficult for my friend to get to know me in ways that she can then use to lead me to greater self-knowledge. This is not impossible, of course, particularly in friendships that retain a large face-to-face component. For example, if Eve has seen Marcus blush whenever Tomas' name has arisen, then Eve might read it as significant that Tomas appears in every photo of a recent party that Marcus posted. Or if Marcy knows that Dana is unhappy about her recent weight gain because she has seen Dana's altered body language, then Marcy will be able to read shame off of the fact that Dana has ceased to post any pictures of herself. But in these cases of Eve interpreting Marcus's posts and Marcy reading those of Dana, the interpretation of social media data is embedded in a background of face-to-face interaction. Without that background, the omnipresence of Tomas in Marcus's photos and Dana's lack of photos of herself might go unnoticed or might lead to very different interpretations from the interpretations arrived at in the context of what has been gleaned from face-to-face interaction.

We might think that being completely open on social media would obviate this obstacle to friendship's production of self-knowledge in its participants. The difficulty, however, is that even if we make every effort to be open, what we are open about is how we see and understand ourselves. Cocking and Kennett rightly emphasize that who we are is in part a product of our interactions with our friends and, in particular, with those friends' interpretations of us, including with their interpretations of our own self-understanding and how that self-understanding fits with what we do and otherwise say. Purely online interactions cut our friends off from being able to perform this task because they are blocked from significant sources of knowledge about us: our body language, how we interact with other people, how we interact with them, changes in body language and interactions (for an example, see the case of Marcy and Dana above), etc.

The barriers to my acquiring self-knowledge via online interaction with a friend are not all on my side: some result from the constraints of responding to another in a semi-public forum. Online responses often take highly conventionalized, minimal forms, such as the use of hashtags, emojis, 'likes,' or very brief messages such as "Way to go!", "Totally!", etc. Validation and agreement are often the leitmotifs of social media interaction, but neither is well-suited to uncovering self-deception or evasion of any sort. And, of course, we can simply block those whose comments we find upsetting in any way. In the face of a host of 'likes' and thumbs-up or smiley-face emojis, it is hard to be honest or to take honesty without defensiveness or offense.

I also think that it is just harder for the necessary honesty to occur in a caring way via text rather than face-to-face. Face-to-face we can moderate what we say with facial expression and body language, with a gentle clasp of the hand or an arm around the shoulders, or with the tone of voice that we use. We can also instantly see how the other is responding to what we say and attempt to head off misinterpretation or pull back on what seems to be coming across as too harsh. This is all very difficult, if not impossible to do with the buffer of technology between two people.

Again, of course, I need to emphasize that these are challenges to using social media in the maintenance of a friendship, and just how challenging they in fact are will depend upon a multitude of factors: the self-awareness of the friends, the amount of face-to-face interaction between the friends, the number of people one is addressing on, for example, one's Facebook page, the nature of the established background of the friendship, etc. But I think that even in mature and well-established friendships, the challenges remain because of some of the primary motivators for the use of social media in the first place: keeping in touch with people when getting together is too difficult or costly, and keeping in touch with a wide range and number of people. The first factor is likely to make us hasty and less thoughtful in our use of social media, while the latter is likely to make us less open and honest (whether posting on our own page or posting on the page of a friend). So while thoughtful use of social media can supplement mature friendships (as in the examples I gave of Marcy and Dana and of Eve and Marcus), such thoughtful use is often antithetical to our very reasons for using social media. Caution is then in order as we attempt to balance social media usage with our face-to-face interactions with friends.

I have already mentioned at the beginning of this section that blocking of access to body language can inhibit the exercise of empathy in our interactions with our friends. Studies have been inconclusive about the link, if any, between the reduction in the empathy of young people and their use of social media.[9] This is an important area for future monitoring and research because of empathy's key role in developing and maintaining friendships and in deriving value from those friendships. We use empathy in making and keeping friends, and in making and keeping friends we further develop our empathetic capacities. If social media usage inhibits the development of these capacities, then such usage is inhibiting young people's ability to build and to derive value from friendships. And, of course, empathy is an important capacity for moral development. So if social media has these results, we need to carefully monitor how young people use it or they might be unable to have valuable friendships in their lives or to develop good moral characters.

5.2 THE SUBJECTIVE AND OBJECTIVE INTRINSIC VALUE OF FRIENDSHIP

In Chapter Four I suggested that most of us have both intrinsic and instrumental desires for friendship where, in that chapter, I was imagining a friendship as taking the traditional form, i.e. as involving primarily face-to-face interaction. We have instrumental desires for friendship primarily in so far as we have intrinsic desires for pleasure, and we see friendship as an important, perhaps essential means to having a significant amount of pleasure in our lives. But we also, I claimed, have intrinsic desires for friendship in so far as we want, for its own sake, to be cared about and to be intimate with someone in the way that is characteristic and definitive of friendship. So satisfying our intrinsic and our instrumental desires requires, for most of us, making friends, and thus, if we hold a desire-satisfaction conception of value, making friends is, for most of us, required for living a good life.

One important effect of technology is the way in which it can alter what we desire or how we understand the objects of our desires. So as we use social media (and text messages and e-mail and Skype) more and more in conducting our interpersonal relationships, what we think of when we think of interactions with friends might alter. Right now, most people, in particular adults, have a fairly clear grasp of the distinction between a friend and a Facebook 'friend,' understanding that the former is not necessarily the latter and vice versa. But we need to maintain caution in order to make sure that what is now a clear line does not become blurred, particularly for those who may never have known what it is to conduct a friendship without the use of social media and other technological applications. Facebook reports to us (and to others) how many 'friends' we have, and many people want to maintain some 'respectable' number of friends. The worry is that this sort of phenomena will lead to our viewing friends more instrumentally, i.e. as means to keeping our count high. We also might come to view our friends as yardsticks for measuring our own possessions and accomplishments, and will then think of them more as rivals as we shape our personas in response to the personas that our friends have crafted online.[10]

Now, none of this would matter to the value of our lives if we accept a desire-satisfaction conception of intrinsic value: as our intrinsic desires change, what has intrinsic value for us changes. Whereas previously we might have intrinsically desired deep intimate connection and affection, we might, as a result of social media usage, come to value brief, convention-alized exchanges that maintain more, but greatly attenuated connections. However, if we alter our desires with respect to how we interact with others, this could have an impact on our ability to satisfy other desires that we have. Thus, if we come to have as a goal relationships with a large online component and we primarily pursue such relationships, then we might have a more difficult time satisfying our desires for pleasure, self-development, self-knowledge, and the avoidance of isolation and loneliness. So even on a desire-satisfaction conception of intrinsic value, a change with respect to the kinds of inter-personal relationships that we desire might lessen the overall value in our lives even if we manage to actually have precisely the kinds of interpersonal relationships that we want to have.

But we might also think that it would be unfortunate if we came to desire different kinds of interpersonal relationships, even if such a shift did not lead to fewer of our other desires being satisfied. If, say, young people desired friendships con-ducted primarily via social media and texting, we might think that they were missing something from their lives, perhaps something that they were unable to appreciate because they had never had, and perhaps did not have the capacity for, more robust intimate connections. Thus, if we held a counterfactual desire-satisfaction conception of intrinsic value, we would be able to insist that if people were competent judges they would intrinsically desire friendship conducted primarily via more traditional, face-to-face modes of interaction. According to such an account of intrinsic value, then, we should find it worrisome if young people do not develop the abilities, such as empathy,[11] necessary for traditional friendship: such young people will not be competent judges and so their own intrin-sic desires will not be guides to living a good life.

However, as I pointed out in Chapter Four, one reason why we might be equating what has intrinsic value with what competent judges would desire is that we think that competent judges are in the best epistemic position for grasping what has objective intrinsic value. And I also pointed out that it is plausible to suppose that friendship has objective intrinsic value. But friendship is a complex state of affairs, involving two people with attitudes of mutual special concern and love or affection (or some other emotion in that ballpark), desires to spend time together, a continuing history of interaction that expresses (and is recognized as expressing) concern, and/or mutual special knowledge. All of these potential components of the friendship relation come in degrees: we have more concern and love or affection, deeper special knowledge, a longer and/or richer history of concerned interaction, and/or stronger desires to be with certain friends than with others. Given that the complex relationship that is friendship has these various components that come in degrees, it is plausible to suppose that the objective intrinsic value of any given friendship will in some way be a function of the value of these components.[12] So an attenuation in some aspect of the friendship is likely to lead to a diminution in intrinsic value, unless, of course, that attenuation is compensated for by an enrichment in some other aspect of the friendship.

Chapter Three considered the ways in which the friendship relation itself might be affected by the use of social media in the conducting of that friendship. We saw that loss of physical presence could result in reduction in the nature and quality of the special knowledge that friends have of each other and reduce intimacy. The comparison-based culture fostered on social media such as Facebook could lead to a diminution in affection and concern in the face of resentment, jealousy, and rivalry. Desires to spend time together could be weakened if we manage to convince ourselves that we can maintain friendships just as easily without the effort of face-to-face contact. If these effects actually occur, then it would seem that the value of the resultant friendships would be reduced in so far as important and valuable components of those friendships have been reduced without any compensating gain in some other valuable aspect of the friendship.

Are there, however, compensating gains? As I have mentioned, one of the most highly touted supposed advantages of Facebook is its ability to keep us connected to geographically distant friends and to reconnect us with those with whom we have lost contact, such as people with whom we went to high school or college. So it might be said, if friendship is valuable, and social media facilitates the sustaining or re-establishing of friendships that otherwise would dissolve or remain dissolved, then social media is adding value to our lives. Thus, even if some friendships have diminution in some aspect such as affection or special knowledge, this diminution is more than made up for by the number of friendships that we can maintain via the use of social media.

How many friends, though, can we actually have? We all know that some of our friends are 'good' friends in the sense of being very close friends, while others are such that we are not particularly close with them. Would an increase in number of the latter sort of friend that we have be able to compensate for the loss of a good friend or for the loss of the closeness that we previously had with a friend? Would having a mutual mild affection with a great number of people be able to compensate me for the loss of a mutual deep love and affection with one person? Would several people having only a moderate special knowledge of me compensate for the loss

Friendship and Social Media

of a friend who had a very rich and deep understanding and knowledge of me?

In terms of the value of consequences, how such trade-offs would work out would, of course, vary from one person to another. So, for example, Sophie might get X units of pleasure from each of ten not-very-close friendships, so that she gets a sum total of 10X units of pleasure. But Sam might get 10X units of pleasure from his very close friendship with Dean. However, I do think that Sophie is highly unlikely to get the same benefits of self-knowledge and self-development from her ten friendships that Sam is likely to get from his friendship with Dean. After all, it is likely that a certain threshold of intimacy needs to be attained before these particular consequences can be gained, and it may be that that level of intimacy is only achieved in quite close friendships.

On the other hand, when it comes to intrinsic value, I am inclined to think that one very close friendship is highly valuable, and it would take an awful lot of mild friendships to compensate for its loss. Here I think that some kind of organic wholes view is likely to be correct. Consider again Sophie's ten, let us call them 'mild,' friendships and Sam's one deep friendship with Dean. We can suppose that if we add up all of the concern and affection in Sophie's ten friendships that it equals the concern and affection between Sam and Dean, and similarly for every other component of the friendship relation. Given that I am inclined to think that Sam and Dean's deep friendship is better than Sophie's ten mild ones, I am inclined to think that having all of the components of the relationship of a deep intensity combined together makes them more valuable than if the components are spread out among a greater number of friendships. If I am right about this, then if online friendships lose depth and intensity we are in danger of reducing the value of our lives, even if we acquire a great many of these 'mild' online friendships.

5.3 BEING CAUTIOUS

I have tried to make clear that any conclusions that we reach about social media usage in friendship must be tentative and speculative at this point. Also, given that friendships differ so much in character and that how people use social media in those friendships also differs quite a bit, this is an area where it is difficult to make any generalizations. However, I think that it is clear that we need to exert caution in exploiting social media in the conducting of our friendships. Chapters Two and Three showed us that, given the nature of friendship, social media usage can pose challenges to maintaining the various components of a friendship. Chapter Four showed us the many ways that friendship makes our lives go better. So if we face the obstacles to achieving that value discussed in the present chapter, then even if we manage to maintain friendships, as we use social media and other technologies, we clearly need to exert caution and careful thought as to how we use them. The difficulty is that we often turn to technologies such as social media because we are busy, we are rushed, we are spread thin, and it is easier to text or post on a friend's Facebook page than to try to find a time to meet for tea. The very reasons, then, that we turn to social media work against our exerting the effort and forethought needed to forestall a weakening of friendship bonds and a loss of value in our lives. We also know that friendship requires practice in so far as it requires capacities such as empathy, and so we need to exert special caution in determining how we let young people conduct their relationships so that they do not lose the capacity for deep intimate connections. Social media and other technologies offer promise in certain ways, but we need to acknowledge the dangers and make sure that we think through these issues so that the dangers do not come to outweigh the promise.

NOTES

1 See the discussion in Chapter Three.
2 For just a sample, see Edson C. Tandoc, Patrick Ferrucci, and Margaret Duffy, "Facebook Use, Envy, and Depression Among College Students: Is Facebooking Depressing?" *Computers in Human Behavior* 43 (2015): 139–146; H.T. Chou and N. Edge, "'They are Happier and Having Better Lives Than I Am': The Impact of Using Facebook on Perceptions of Others' Lives," *Cyberpsychology, Behavior, and Social Networking* 15(2) (2015): 117–121; and X. Hu, A. Kim, N. Siwek, and D. Wilder, "The Facebook Paradox: Effects of Facebooking on Individuals' Social Relationships and Psychological Well-Being," *Frontiers in Psychology*, January 31, 2017.
3 Advertising, of course, functions by way of playing upon this kind of comparison-induced sense of inferiority. We see the great lives of people in print and TV ads, recognize that our own lives fall short of such depictions, and are then, supposedly, led to buy the products advertised in order to get our own lives to approximate those of the happy people in the ads.
4 This, of course, recalls the debate between Cocking and Matthews and Briggle that I discussed in Chapter Three. For Briggle's claims to be plausible, I believe, we have to limit their scope to the use of the one-on-one features of social media, i.e. to the ones least often used.
5 There is a lot of conflicting data on this matter, depending on the nature of the sample population in a given study. For an example see Hayeon Song, Anne Zmyslinski-Seelig, Jinyoung Kim, Adam Drent, Angela Victor, Kikuko Amori, and Mike Allen, "Does Facebook Make You Lonely? A Meta Analysis," *Computers in Human Behavior* 36 (2014): 446–452.
6 I do not want to be taken as denying that there might be other causes of loneliness, including some deep existential sense of the meaninglessness of human existence or a sense of one's own mortality. What I am pointing to is what I take to be perhaps a more mundane, but certainly a more common, cause of loneliness.
7 See Holly Stead and Peter A. Bibby, "Personality, Fear of Missing Out and Problematic Internet Use and Their Relationship to Subjective Well-Being," *Computers in Human Behavior* 76 (2017): 534–540. For a study linking these negative feelings to broader use of technology, see Jon D.

Elhai, Jason C. Levine, Robert D. Dvorak, and Brian J. Hall, "Fear of Missing Out, Need for Touch, Anxiety and Depression are Related to Problematic Smartphone Use," *Computers in Human Behavior* 63 (2016): 509–516.

8 Just use Google and you will see how many links there are about how to deal with people who do not respond to texts, how to understand what a lack of response means, etc.

9 See L. Mark Carrier, Alexander Spradlin, John P. Bunce, and Larry D. Rosen, "Virtual Empathy: Positive and Negative Effects of Going Online Upon Empathy in Young Adults," *Computers in Human Behavior* 52 (2015): 39–48.

10 For a disturbing examination of taking the ratings and comparisons of social media to an extreme, see the *Black Mirror* episode "Nosedive" (directed by Joe Wright, written by Mike Schur and Rashida Jones) in which people rank each other on every encounter and these rankings determine everything in one's life.

11 Empathy is a crucial capacity for friendship, of course, but also for moral development and character. So any suggestion that social media usage can affect negatively users' empathy is highly troubling.

12 Although, as we saw in Chapter Four's discussion of organic wholes, we cannot presume that that function will be straightforwardly additive.

Index

advantage, friendship for 28–9, 32
anhedonia 118
Aristotle: on friendship 7, 31, 121;
    on solitude 1; on virtue 14, 31

Bentham, J., on pleasure 120
biography, social media as 80
Brandt, R. 115
Briggle, A. 72, 73, 139
buffer: digital 73; social media
    as 139

Cocking, D. and Kennett, J.: "Friendship
    and Moral Danger" 46–7;
    "Friendship and the Self" 40–1
Cocking, D. and Matthews, S. 71, 73,
    136, 145
contingent truths 7; friendship as 13;
    see also necessary truths

Death in Brunswick (film) 47, 103
'defriend' x, 3, 25
Delaney, D. 32
depression 118–19; and
    Facebook 137
desire, and intrinsic value 111
desire-satisfaction: counterfactual
    115–16, 121; and friends 110–17;
    and intrinsic value 112, 149–50
digital buffer 73

e-mail ix, 2, 65, 75, 149
embodiment, in friendship 69, 77,
    81–2
empathy: and face-to-face interaction
    76–7, 145; and friendship 75–6,
    88n7, 109, 156n11
envy, and Facebook 137, 142

face-to-face interaction: and empathy
    76–7, 145; and friendship 79–80;
    vs text contact 147
Facebook 2; being ignored on
    143; and depression 137; and
    envy 137, 142; and friendship
    3, 25, 152; and loneliness 140;
    and unhappiness 84–5; and
    well-being 84
'Facebook friends' 137, 149; pen
    friendship, comparison 25
family, and friendship 55–6
family relationships, and friendship
    60–2
frenemies 25–6; conflicted
    relationships 26–7, 33–4, 54;
    and friendship 42–4, 110; and
    insecurity 34–5; self-disclosure
    39–40; and trust 46
'friend request' 25
friendlessness 121–2; see also
    loneliness; solitude

friends: vs acquaintances 85–6; close 94–5; companionable silence among 53; and desire-satisfaction 110–17; on Facebook 137; knowledge of 70–5; *Necessity of Friends* 8, 9, 10, 90; non-desire for 114; pros and cons 12–13; reasons for wanting 110–14; special obligations to 58–9; value of 10–13, 89–91, 133; *see also* 'Facebook friends; friendship

friendship: for advantage 28–9, 32; Aristotle on 7, 31, 121; boundaries 74–5; and caring interaction 40–2; "Charlie's" story 7, 8–9; and choice 55–6; close 74; complete 29, 31, 58, 65, 81, 87n1; as contingent truth 13; continuum of 66; definition 26; differences 74; embodiment in 69, 77, 81–2; and empathy 75–6, 88n7, 109, 156n11; and face-to-face interaction 79–80; and Facebook 3, 25, 152; and family 55–6; and family relationships 60–2; and frenemies 42–4, 110; garden maintenance metaphor 68; 'good' 94; and the good life 2, 7, 19, 123, 126; instrumental value 92; as intimacy 50–7, 86, 144; intrinsic value 13, 92–4, 113, 117–19, 123, 148–9, 151; isolation test 93; for its own sake 30–1; lasting 31; and loneliness 122, 141–2; and love 48–50; and marriage 62; and moral character 19, 44–8, 104–5, 126, 126–8; and moral commitment 27, 59; and morality 13–19, 47–8; and necessity 4–7; and organic wholes 122–5,

153–4; philosophers of 51; and pleasure 29, 32, 63n4, 99, 100–1, 103, 113, 133–4; and rationality 128–30; risks 102–3, 130; and self-disclosure 36–40, 44, 50–1; and self-knowledge 107–9, 136, 144–6; and self-understanding 105; and sexual relationships 62; shared activities 53; and shared knowledge 78–9; and social media 68–9, 77–8, 147, 151–2; and technology 26, 149; and trust 36, 41, 136; *see also* friends

Gauthier, D. 14
the good life: concept 19–20, 20–1; and friendship 2, 7, 19, 123, 126

happiness, concept 20
Hedonism 20; paradox 99, 131n3; and value 98; *see also* pleasure
Hobbes, T.: on morality 14; on self-interest 14, 111

insecurity, and frenemies 34–5
Instagram 2, 65
intimacy: friendship as 50–7, 86, 144; nature of 86–7; social media impact 67
intrinsic value: and desire 111, 151; and desire-satisfaction 112, 149–50; friendship 13, 92–4, 113, 117–19, 123, 148–9, 151
isolation, and loneliness 142

Kant, I., on pleasure 23n7
King, C., "You've Got a Friend" 3
knowledge: Plato on 106; *see also* self-knowledge; shared knowledge

'LOL', reactions to 83–4

loneliness: in a crowd 140; and Facebook 140; and friendship 122, 141–2; and isolation 142; nature of 140–1; and social media 140; *see also* friendlessness; solitude

love, and friendship 48–50

marriage, and friendship 62

Mill, John Stuart: *The Subjection of Women* 62; *Utilitarianism* 114

money, value of 12

moral character, and friendship 19, 44–8, 104–5, 126–8

moral commitment, and friendship 27, 59

morality: and friendship 13–19, 47–8; Hobbes on 14; Plato on 14

necessary truths 6–7; *see also* contingent truths

necessity: concept 5–7; and friendship 4–7

Necessity of Friends 8, 9, 10, 90

organic wholes, and friendship 122–5, 153–4

Plato: on knowledge 106; on morality 14; on pleasure 12, 23n7

pleasure: Bentham on 120; and friendship 29, 32, 63n4, 99, 100–1, 103, 113, 133–4; indirect approach to 99; intensity of 120; as intrinsically good 12, 97, 98; Kant on 23n7; Plato on 12, 23n7; of solitude 124, 140; *see also* anhedonia; Hedonism

rationality, and friendship 128–30

Reiman, J. H. 86

risks, friendship 102–3, 130

self-disclosure: frenemies 39–40; and friendship 36–40, 44, 50–1

self-interest, Hobbes on 14, 111

self-knowledge, and friendship 107–9, 136, 144–6

self-presentation, on social media 71–2, 136–7, 138–9

self-revelation *see* self-disclosure

self-understanding, and friendship 105

sexual relationships, and friendship 62

shared knowledge, and friendship 78–9

Skype ix, 2, 53, 65, 75, 149

social media: as biography 80; as buffer 139; and friendship 68–9, 77–8, 147, 151–2; limitations 84, 87, 154–5; and loneliness 140; photos/videos 84; self-presentation on 71–2, 136–7, 138–9; and trust 138; *see also* Facebook

solitude: Aristotle on 1; pleasure of 124, 140; *see also* friendlessness; loneliness

Stockholm syndrome 55, 56

technology, and friendship 26, 149

The Third Man (film) 82–3, 102

Thomas, L. 27, 36, 44, 46, 50

trust: and frenemies 46; and friendship 36, 41, 136; and social media 138

truths *see* contingent truths; necessary
   truths
Twitter xii, 2, 65, 80, 84, 134, 143

unhappiness, and Facebook use 84–5

Vallor, S. 68, 144
valuable life, concept 20–1

value: and hedonism 98;
intrinsic vs instrumental 11–12, 92;
   see also intrinsic value
of money 12; subjective vs objective
   95–6; *see also under* friendship
virtue, Aristotle on 14, 31

well-being, and Facebook 84

Printed in the United States
by Baker & Taylor Publisher Services